WRITE YOUR *heart* OUT

REBECCA McCLANAHAN

WALKING STICK PRESS
Cincinnati, Ohio
http://www.writersdigest.com

Write Your Heart Out: Exploring and Expressing What Matters to You.
Copyright © 2001 by Rebecca McClanahan. Manufactured in the United States
of America. All rights reserved. No part of this book may be reproduced in any
form or by any electronic or mechanical means including information storage
and retrieval systems without permission in writing from the publisher, except
by a reviewer, who may quote brief passages in a review. Published by Walking
Stick Press, an imprint of F&W Publications, Inc., 1507 Dana Avenue, Cincinnati,
Ohio 45207. (800) 289-0963. First edition.

Visit our Web site at http://www.writersdigest.com for information on more resources for writers.

To receive a free weekly e-mail newsletter delivering tips and updates about
writing and about Writer's Digest products, register directly at our Web site at
http://newsletters.fwpublications.com.

05   04   03   02   01   5   4   3   2   1

Library of Congress Cataloging-in-Publication Data

McClanahan, Rebecca
        Write your heart out / by Rebecca McClanahan.
        p.   cm.
        ISBN 1-58297-006-8
        1. English language—Rhetoric. 2. Creative writing. I. Title.

PE1408.M265   2001
808'.042—dc21   2001026834
                                                        CIP

Edited by Jack Heffron and Kim Agricola
Designed by Angela Lennert Wilcox
Cover designed by Andrea Short
Cover photograph: © Kamil Vojnar/Photonica
Production coordinated by Emily Gross

PRAISE FOR REBECCA
McCLANAHAN'S WORKS
ON *Word Painting*

"Here is splendid advice for poets and prose writers alike, in vivid sentences that illustrate the book's themes."
—Doris Betts, author of *Beasts of the Southern Wild and Other Stories* and *The Sharp Teeth of Love: A Novel*

"The advice in *Word Painting* is like Rebecca McClanahan's writing style: clear, concise, fresh, elegant."
—Clyde Edgerton, author of *Walking Across Egypt, In Memory of Junior,* and *Where Trouble Sleeps*

"Too many writers have considered description as being more background for, or ornament to, their stories. McClanahan not only demonstrates its organic necessity but shows ways in which it can be made more vital, more exciting, and simply more enjoyable than I had imagined possible."
—Fred Chappell, author of *Farewell, I'm Bound to Leave You, More Shapes Than One,* and *Brighten the Corner Where You Are*

"This is the best teaching tool I have bought in years."
—Cecile Goding, Iowa City, Iowa

"This book has been a godsend to me. It's been enormously helpful in doing the final edit of my novel. Reading it made me feel like I had my own personal editor. It showed me many things I would have never learned on my own."
—Karon Luddy, Charlotte, North Carolina

"When people come into the Gothic and ask me for a book to help them develop their creative writing, I always recommend *Word Painting*. It is the best book I know of for poetry and prose writers, at whatever level, to assist them in shaping their craft."

—Elon G. Eidenier, Assistant director,
Duke University Stores, The Gothic Bookshop

O N   *T h e   I n t e r s e c t i o n   o f   X   a n d   Y*

"A quiet, powerful book—like good southern bourbon—about lovers and families and all those unexpected turns our lives take."

—Dave Smith, Editor, *The Southern Review*

"These open-eyed poems, scanting no loss or error we have made, are full of the stunned pleasure of being alert, and offer that gift to their lucky readers."

—William Matthews

O N   *M r s .   H o u d i n i*

"No one has written poems of the feminine experience that are less strident or more profoundly political."

—Rodney Jones

O N   *N a k e d   a s   E v e*

"A consummate poet, McClanahan proves herself a master at achieving just the right tone of voice, somber or high-spirited; the appearance of *Naked as Eve*, her fourth collection, is an occasion to gladden the heart."

—Colette Inez

for

CAROLYN BEST SCHIRMER

FRIEND AND MENTOR

1924 – 1996

ACKNOWLEDGMENTS

Few writing projects are conceived, drafted, revised, and completed by a writer working in isolation. Most require at least some collaboration, even if the project bears only one name. *Write Your Heart Out* is the result of my collaboration with dozens of people, some of whom are not identified by name within these pages. Many shared their writing experiences with me; many sent poems, essays, and stories; some suggested bibliographical references; and a few even composed material specifically for this book. To all these people, I extend my heartfelt thanks.

In particular, I wish to thank Janice Eidus, Gail Peck, and Susan Thames for their honest, thorough, and tactful criticism of the manuscript and for their ongoing support of my work. I'm also indebted to Melanie Peter and Dede Wilson, whose generous and eloquent accounts of grief provided the basis for chapter five. I extend special thanks to my editor, Jack Heffron, who suggested that I write this book and saw it through to completion. And, as always, I thank my husband, Donald Devet, who sustains me with love, patience, and an inimitable sense of humor.

DONALD DEVET

Rebecca McClanahan has published four books of poetry, most recently *Naked as Eve* (Copper Beech Press), as well as *Word Painting: A Guide to Writing More Descriptively* (Writer's Digest Books), and *One Word Deep* (Ashland Poetry Press) a book of lectures and readings. In 2002, the University of Georgia Press will publish her book of essays, *The Riddle Song and Other Mysteries*. McClanahan's work has been anthologized in *The Pushcart Prize XVIII*, *The Best American Poetry 1998*, and *The Best American Essays 2001*. It has also appeared in numerous periodicals including *Boulevard*, *The Georgia Review*, *The Gettysburg Review*, and *The Kenyon Review*. She has received a PEN/Syndicated Fiction Award, the J. Howard and Barbara M.J. Wood Prize from *Poetry*, the Carter Prize for nonfiction from *Shenandoah*, and a Governor's Award for Excellence in Education. McClanahan has taught writing for over twenty-five years and currently lives in New York City.

CONTENTS

INTRODUCTION

By the time you read these words, they will have flown through space and time from my hand to yours; there will be nothing more for me to do. So as I write I try to imagine you out there, months or years from now. I see you scanning the bookstore shelf, taking this volume down, running your hand across its cover, wondering what it means to "write your heart out." You're looking for something—I can't be sure just what. I close my eyes and imagine:

- Ever since you were a child, people have been saying you have a way with words.
- Your parents are growing old, and you don't want their stories to get lost.
- Phrases come to you unannounced, begging to become poems.
- At night you can't sleep; all day your mind races. You wonder if writing might calm you.
- You've kept a journal for years and would like to enlarge your writing options.
- Something wonderful has happened. You'll burst if you can't share it.
- Something terrible has happened, and you survived to tell about it.
- You've always said you would write a novel someday.
- Your writing hand is starting to itch.

Maybe you're just beginning your writing journey. You've glimpsed the muse, shrugging her smooth lovely shoulders and beckoning for you to follow. You may be wondering what's in store for you, where the journey might lead. Or maybe you've been on the journey a long time. Whether you're a beginner or a continuer, writing offers rewards that few other activities can offer:

1. Writing provides a record of people, places, events,

and emotions that might otherwise be lost. You may think you'll never forget how your child called bread crumbs "bum creds" or the way frost tipped the edges of the maples the day your father died or the pungent aroma of the hot chestnuts you unwrapped just yesterday on a New York street. Chances are you will. Writing is, in part, an attempt to save your life (and other lives) from extinction. Even if you choose to write entirely from your imagination, your writing will serve as a record of one mind's journey through this world. The story you wrote yesterday—or the poem, essay, or journal entry—is a letter mailed from the past to the present. And the story you write today is a time capsule sealed for the future.

2. Writing slows you down. Like yoga, meditation, good sex, or a fabulous meal, writing stops you in your tracks. It's hard to be somewhere else when you're writing. You can hurry through life most of the time—switching lanes, punching buttons, pointing and clicking on computer icons, skimming words someone else has written. But writing fastens you to the present moment, providing a space for thought and reflection.

3. Although writing cannot shield you from confusion, failure, loss, or despair, it can help reshape the pain. The healing power of writing cannot be overstated. As your hand moves across the page, you can almost feel your grief growing a body and acquiring a voice. Soon it outgrows your private memory and strikes out on its own, searching for a larger context. When this happens, what you had previously recalled only as an ache, a tightness in your chest, is transformed. The slap across your face works its way into a story, thereby losing some of its sting. All you thought you couldn't bear feels bearable after all.

4. The act of writing clarifies emotions and motives, dispels demons, and enables you to "talk" your way to possible solutions. Writing provides a form for the chaos, a place

to put the undistilled thoughts and feelings that otherwise cloud our lives. Writing is, in the words of Audre Lorde, "the way we help give name to the nameless so it can be thought."

5. Writing keeps you from tiring of the world. A bit of overheard conversation which you might otherwise ignore attaches itself to the essay you're working on; a yellow mitten, dropped by a child on the playground, provides the missing image for the song you've been writing. When you're engaged in a writing task, the beam of your attention narrows and the ordinary is made new—or so it appears to your newly focused eyes.

6. To name the world in your own terms, to tell your own story, is an act of authority and power. When you write, you are saying, in effect, "I have a voice. I have a story. This is what I have to say."

7. Writing is like hosting a party where all the people you have known, been, or imagined show up at the door. Your past selves pour in through a hole in time; your grandmother steps through space and sits on the edge of the desk; and the red-haired toddler you'd glimpsed only in dreams appears fully dressed in the middle of your poem, wearing the corduroy vest you knitted out of scraps of nouns, verbs, and prepositions. Amazing.

8. Although each act of writing may not necessarily make you a better writer, it makes you better prepared for the next act of writing. "A writer," wrote William Stafford, "is not so much someone who has something to say as he is someone who has found a process that will bring about new things he would not have thought of if he had not started to say them." Writing begets more writing; meaning grows on the page.

9. If you choose to share what you've written, your words might change a reader's life; your story might be just the story someone needs to read. And even if you choose not

to share your work, your words will nevertheless have an impact on one reader: you. The life you save, as Flannery O'Connor once suggested, might be your own.

10. When you write, you align yourself with others who are engaged in the same strange, exhilarating pursuit. Although you may sometimes feel alone as you sit at your desk trying to release the next phrase from your pen, you aren't alone. At the same instant, hundreds of thousands of writers are sitting at their desks or kitchen tables, speaking into tape recorders, or pacing the floor searching for a word (perhaps the very word you're searching for). A grandmother in South Dakota is writing a mystery; a teenager in Philadelphia is scratching out a poem; a Nobel prize–winning author, grieving for past successes, is staring out the window wondering how in the world the next sentence will appear. We're all in this together, even the dead writers who left their words like crumbs for us to follow. We're a family, a guild of artisans, a brotherhood, a sisterhood, a motley crew, and yes—of course—there are a few rotten apples in the bunch. But mostly we mean well. We're all just trying to tell our story.

Part of my story is this book, which I wrote as a guide for anyone—including me—wishing to write with honesty, passion, imagination, and heart. *Write Your Heart Out* grew out of a personal need not only to articulate what I already knew I knew about writing but also to discover what I didn't yet know I knew. (That's a whopper of a sentence, I realize, but it says exactly what it's supposed to say.) Writing the book was a process which felt, at times, like excavation: Word by word, paragraph by paragraph, what I needed to say was slowly revealed.

Writing the book was also an act of rediscovery—a renewing of vows, so to speak. In the process of writing about my life's work, old truths were made new again, and I was reminded of why I began writing my heart out in the first place, all those years ago. We write, in part, the words we need to read. I needed to read this book, but first I needed to write it.

Write Your Heart Out is organized like a spiral, a shape that reflects the book's evolution. The spiral begins at the axis of personal need, the "private I," and spins out, chapter by chapter, into what I call the "public eye." The early sections of the book are concerned with uncovering your heart's truths, discovering authentic subjects, writing with honesty and authority, and developing the habits of a writer. As the book moves on, I discuss writing as a method for navigating challenging life passages, recording memories, expressing emotion, building community, and transforming personal experiences through the imagination. Finally, we look at ways to revise and reshape your writing for an outside audience, preparing your "private I" to meet the "public eye." *Write Your Heart Out* is a mixture of direct instruction, writing exercises and prompts, examples from published and unpublished texts, and personal reflections on the writing process.

Many books about writing focus on particular literary forms—poetry, plays, novels, short stories, or essays. Others deal solely with issues of craft—how to build stronger plots, write clearer sentences, and create believable characters. Although I occasionally address issues of craft and suggest techniques that apply to particular genres, my primary emphasis within these pages is writing as process rather than as product. I emphasize writing as a form of exploration, a way not merely to communicate what you already know but also to uncover new thoughts, feelings, ideas, subjects, and imaginative connections.

"Writing your heart out" suggests self-discovery as well as self-expression. It also suggests writing with passion, energy, and commitment. To this end, I stress the importance of integrating writing into your life by practicing a discipline that suits your goals, temperament, and life circumstances. The writing life, though exhilarating and rewarding, is not always easy; and I've tried to be honest about the difficulties as well as the rewards, the valleys as well as the peaks. Once you take the first step, your journey as a writer will begin. I hope this book will help guide you through the terrain.

CHAPTER 1

WHY WE DON'T WRITE

OUR HEARTS OUT

As I write these words, a jackhammer is breaking open the sidewalk outside my apartment, I am groggy from nightmares of tunnels and root canals, the freezer in my ancient refrigerator is exhaling yet another cloud of ice, my e-mail is backing up, the laundry is piling up, and the light on my answering machine is blinking the number five.

There are so many reasons not to write, it's a miracle this sentence appears.

Several years ago, during a period when I seemed unable to get to the desk, I made a list of all the reasons why I couldn't/shouldn't/wouldn't write. It was the best thing I'd written in months. My heart was really in it. As it turns out, there are dozens of reasons not to write: We are too old or too young. We don't have enough education, experience, or talent. We have no ideas. Our spelling is atrocious. If only we didn't have jobs, if we didn't have children, if we weren't so tired, if we lived on the beach or in the mountains instead of in this jackhammering city, if someone would read what we write, if only someone would publish it.

It will do no good to decide we're going to write if we don't first ask ourselves why we haven't been doing it all along. When I read back over my list, I discover that most of my reasons aren't reasons at all. They're well-founded excuses, firmly rooted in misconceptions. Misconceptions about writing are held most firmly by those who don't write or who plan one day to write or who are sure they could write a best-seller if they just put their mind to it. But misconceptions are also held by those of us who write regularly and have been writing most of our lives. Here are some of the misconceptions that serve me well when I'm looking for reasons not to write:

Misconception # 1. Writing gets done without writing.
I usually don't answer the phone during my writing hours, but when I do, it's often a friend or family member calling, and the conversation goes something like this:

"Hi. What are you doing?"

"Writing," I answer.

"Really?" she says, as if this were news, as if it weren't the same answer I've been giving for years now. We talk a while, she tells me about her day, I complain about the essay that's tying me in knots, or I exalt in the final revision of a poem that's been eluding me all summer. We say goodbye and hang up.

A week or two later she calls again.

"Hi. What are you doing?"

"Writing."

Again she seems surprised. We talk a while, we say goodbye, and after a few minutes of sharpening pencils (I don't even use pencils) or fantasizing about a six-figure advance on some book I'll never begin or staring out the window where people with real jobs and leather briefcases are hurrying to meetings, I get back to work. Later in the week while I'm getting a haircut, my stylist asks if I'm still writing—as if it were a bad habit, like smoking, that I surely must have kicked by now. It occurs to me to ask him if he's still cutting hair, but I decide that would be mean-spirited. Besides, it takes energy to talk, and I need all my energy for the chapter revision that's backing up in my head. So I just look in the mirror and nod politely.

Even writer friends occasionally seem surprised to find me writing, just as I'm sometimes amazed to catch them in the act. I realize this makes no sense. How else do I suppose their poems, stories, essays, songs, lectures, and journal entries get written? Yet the fantasy that writing gets done without writing is so appealing, it's a hard one to release—like the notion of babies being delivered pain free, via stork or cabbage leaf. While you watch the freshly polished baby asleep in a blanket beside his exhausted mother, it's easy to forget that just hours ago he was a squirming sack of blood and skin and primal scream. And when you read someone else's published novel—or finished poem, short story, or essay—it's hard to imagine the often tedious, painful, messy, sometimes joyous, always life-changing process by which it was delivered, kicking and screaming, into the light.

Like sex or childbirth, writing is almost always a private act. Others don't see us doing it, and the popular media do little to dispel the notion that writing gets done without writing. In movies about writers, the writers do everything but write. They sit in dark cafes, dance on tables, smoke one thin black cigarette after another, slap their lovers, drive too fast, or drink too much. In the few scenes where they're actually writing, the camera doesn't linger. Who would pay seven dollars to watch someone sit at a desk and write? So the camera seeks out something more interesting—the bottle of scotch, the unmade bed, the cocktail dress dropped on the floor—and moves on. One quick shot of the writer's hand on the keyboard (typing, what else, "The End") and he's heading for the door, grabbing the finished manuscript and cigarettes on his way out.

No wonder we imagine writing gets done without writing. And no wonder we believe anyone can write a book. The truth is, anyone *can't* write a book. Only the person who writes a book can write a book.

Misconception # 2. Writers have time to write.
For many people, writing is not an option. Those who are locked in the jaws of war, illness, poverty, violence, illiter-

acy, starvation, or natural or unnatural disasters don't have the luxury of writing. Getting from one day to the next is all they can manage.

On the other end of the spectrum are those for whom life affords every luxury. Blessed with health, talent, opportunities, and material resources, their only responsibility is to the blank page or canvas. Some are born into wealth and privilege; their days are and will always be truly theirs, to use as they will. Others, through cosmic collisions of luck and fate, are granted uninterrupted time and space in which to work. If they choose to write their hearts out, nothing can stop them—or so it appears. (We'll talk more about this assumption later.)

The rest of us fall somewhere between these extremes. And though we cite plenty of reasons for not writing, lack of time seems to be the biggest factor. Listen in on any group of writers long enough, and chances are the subject of time will come up. "If I just had more time," someone sighs aloud, and everyone around the table nods agreement: the poet/single mother of three, the essayist/computer programmer, the novelist/college student, the mystery writer/nurse, the memoirist/carpenter.

The challenge of making time to write is not new, nor is it trivial. For centuries, writers have felt time's weight pressing down upon them, and many have collapsed beneath it. Books, journals, diaries, and interviews are filled with their struggles. In Tillie Olsen's meticulously detailed *Silences*, which ironically marked the end of Olsen's own twenty-year literary silence, she tells of famous and unknown writers alike whose work was interrupted, postponed, abandoned, or, in some cases, barely begun. As Olsen explains, time wasn't the only pressure bearing down on these writers, but it was one of the heaviest. Heavy enough to silence Melville's prose for thirty years while he wore himself out at the customs dock trying to make ends meet. Heavy enough to force Katherine Anne Porter to spend twenty constantly interrupted years writing *Ship of Fools* rather than the two years she estimated it would have taken had she been able to write full-time.

Any piece of writing requires time, and a sustained, artistic, well-crafted creation requires not only actual writing time but time for imagining, thinking, feeling, dreaming, revising, reconsidering, and beginning again. The circumstances of our lives eat up that time; that's why we call them time-consuming. Some time-consuming circumstances are welcome: playing with our children, making dinner for friends, planting a flower garden, taking a trip to the mountains. Other circumstances, if not always welcome, are nevertheless necessary: going to work, filling out tax forms, changing the oil filter, making the grocery list. But whether welcome or unwelcome, pleasant or unpleasant, necessary to our physical survival or to our emotional well-being, these circumstances use up time, time that is not being used for writing.

When day-to-day circumstances absorb the time that could/should/might be used for writing, you may get a little edgy. You might even get angry or envious, imagining living the life of a "real writer": someone who doesn't have to work at another job (or two or three) to make ends meet, who doesn't have to mow the lawn, call the plumber, take out the garbage, clean the chimney, make breakfast, grade papers, feed the kids and the cat. I've wasted whole afternoons doing that old two-step, The Sulk & Carry. (The steps are simple: You just sulk awhile, then carry it with you all day.) It's just not fair, I tell myself. In addition to everything else they have, "real writers" have time to write.

Or so it appears on the surface.

In actuality, no person, however rich or free of outside constraints, has time to write. True, some people have more money, energy, opportunity, or freedom from day-to-day duties than the rest of us. But nature abhors a vacuum, and each life, however privileged, must fill with something. And fill it does. By itself, all the time in the world will not make writing happen. Or, as we've said before, writing only happens by writing, and only the person who writes the book can write the book.

OK, so maybe it won't be a whole book—not this year, anyway. Maybe what you'll manage is a poem a year, one long letter on each grandchild's birthday, a handful of travel essays or short stories, a stack of editorials written to your local newspaper, song lyrics for your daughter's wedding, one wild and crazy screenplay, or a locked diary filled with your secret fears and wishes. Whether you end up publishing a body of work that makes Joyce Carol Oates's output look paltry or writing one story that no one but yourself ever sees is beside the point. The point is, you're writing.

As the Rolling Stones song says, "You can't always get what you want . . . but if you try sometime, you just might find you'll get what you need." If you can make time to read this book, you can make time to write. If you can make time to watch the evening news or your favorite sitcom, you can make time to write. True, you may not be able to make the time you want, but you can make the time you need. You may even find that time limits actually feed the writing process. (We'll discuss this in the next chapter.)

Most of us already have everything we need to do the kind of writing we need to do. And if we don't yet have what we need, there are ways to go about getting it. We can change the external circumstances of our lives to allow more time for writing, we can wait for our circumstances to change, or we can learn to work within the restraints imposed upon us. But one thing is certain: If we spend time complaining that we have no time, we'll have even less time to write.

Misconception # 3. Writers know in advance exactly where they're going, and they get there.
Some writers claim to carry whole books in their heads the way Mozart carried whole sonatas, releasing the finished composition in one swift, turbulent flourish. Some say they know, even before the first word is written, exactly how the story will open, the plot thicken, the theme develop, and all the loose ends tie together on the last page.

As for me—and dozens of writers I know personally and hundreds whose journals, letters, interviews, and memoirs I've studied—writing appears to be an ongoing act of discovery, or, as John Updike says, "a constant search for what one is saying." Some writers begin in the dark, with only a word, a phrase, a cloudy image, or an emotion to guide them; they feel their way to the light. Some, like Katherine Anne Porter, who said she always knew where she was going and how her stories would end, write the ending first and then, in Porter's words, "go back and work towards it," thus making a kind of backward discovery. Still others map out a plan but quickly discard it when the road unexpectedly veers off in a more intriguing direction.

The idea that writers always know in advance exactly where they're going is linked to the first idea we discussed—that writing gets done without writing. Since most writers publish only their final, edited version of a piece of writing, if indeed they publish it at all, readers are rarely able to glimpse a writer's path toward a completed draft. We can't see the crumpled pages, the crossed-out and deleted text, the discarded chapters that were fed to the fire or used to line the parakeet's cage. Because we see only the finished product of a writer's labor, it's easy to assume that everything happened according to plan. Thus, the myth is perpetuated: Writers know exactly where they're going, and they get there.

Misconception # 4. Writers have something important to say.

There's that phrase again: *Writers have*. In our earlier discussion, what writers have is time; now what they have is something important to say. This notion is a double-edged sword. The first edge—that writers *have something*—suggests that writers already possess something whole and complete in itself, before any word is written. Since this something (call it an idea, concept, character, emotion, story, vision) is already fully formed, the writer's job becomes simply putting this something into words.

Put into words. This phrase says much about how the writing process is often perceived. *Put into words* suggests that language is merely the container, the holding bin, into which something is placed. If I just had a great story to tell, so this theory goes, I could tell it. If I could just work out the kinks in this idea, the hard part would be done; then all I'd have to do is write it.

When we buy into this notion, we rob ourselves of the permission to begin without knowing exactly where we're going, we rob the something of its chance to grow and change, and we rob language of its chance to help shape and reshape that something. When we buy into this notion, words become powerless. They hold no sway. They are merely the box into which we place our already perfectly complete thought, story, or vision.

Is it any wonder we despair? Some of us, having decided in advance that our words will never be able to carry the weight of what we want to say, never write the first word. And even those who manage to break through the wall of initial doubt often get no farther than a first draft. We have failed to capture our grandfather, the yellow kitchen, the black dog. We haven't written the poem that seemed so clear in our minds or the story that appeared in our dreams. If only I could find the right words, we think, as if the dictionary were at fault. Or we blame ourselves: We are just not up to the task. Someone else would be able to *put into words* this vision I have. We may begin to question whether what we have to say is worth the paper it's written on.

This leads us to the other edge of this double-sided sword: Writers have something *important* to say. What do we mean by *important*? Well, it depends on whom you ask.

Tolstoy, in *What Is Art?*, suggests that in addition to its other qualities, art is *a new idea that is important to mankind.* Yikes, I think. That's one big shoe to fill. Maybe I shouldn't even try.

Commercial publishers would have us believe we have something important to say if someone is willing to buy it.

And some writers believe what they have to say is important simply because something of import—by which they mean unusual, strange, horrible, or noteworthy—happens to them. But if this is the case, why do we abandon, often after only a few pages, a book written by someone who sailed around the world or broke an Olympic record or murdered her husband or had affairs with three presidents, yet keep going back to that same little story on our shelf, the one about an old woman who does nothing more than take a walk to town?

"Wait a minute," you might be saying. "I've read *A Worn Path*, and you're not playing fair. Eudora Welty could write about a shoelace and make it seem important." Well, maybe you're right. Maybe a great writer can nudge a seemingly trivial something to the ranks of greatness merely through the force of her words.

Or maybe, just maybe, the process is a group effort, a three-member committee composed of Eudora, a something, and the words. Maybe no one is totally in charge; maybe they all just sit around the table and listen to one another. Really listen. The something talks for a while, then language comes in and mixes things up, then Eudora comes in to smooth out the wrinkles, but while she's talking, the something pipes up again. This goes on all morning and into the afternoon, but by the time the three of them knock off for the day, a plan is in motion. And if they keep at it, by the next day (or week or year), the business will be accomplished. Perhaps not in the manner any of the three might have imagined beforehand. Still, the work gets done. And it's none too shabby, they agree, walking out the door together, turning off the light. None too shabby at all.

Misconception # 5. Writers publish their work and get famous or rich or both.

When people ask me what I do for a living, I try to change the subject. If they persist, I tell them that I teach writing, judge writing contests, edit manuscripts, and give lectures and readings. These are not lies; I do all these things. They are, in fact, what I do for a living—that is, to pay the rent and health insurance. What I do for a *life* is write, and that's the part that's hard to explain. I feel the way Louis Armstrong must have felt when he was asked to define jazz. "If you have to ask," he answered, "nothing I say's gonna help."

One of the problems with admitting that you're a writer is that people invariably want to know what you write. Or maybe they don't want to know, but at least they ask. It doesn't work to answer "words." Sometimes, if we're lucky and if we keep putting words on the page, poems or stories or novels or essays eventually emerge, but we don't really write those. What we write is one word, then the next and the next. Seen this way, writing is a very democratic pursuit. It's like the old line about how the president puts on his pants: one leg at a time, just like you, just like me. Seen this way, a Nobel laureate writes the same way a first grader does: one word at a time.

But as I said, this answer doesn't go over well at cocktail

parties. So you mumble something like "poems," hoping to put an end to it.

"Oh really," they say. "What kind?"

Now you've done it. What are you supposed to answer? Long poems? Short? Serious? Free verse? Poems about wilted lettuce, dying dogs, rivers? "Very bad poems," I might answer right now, thinking of the draft I'm currently struggling with.

The conversation can go anywhere from here, but usually it moves in one of these directions:

"My wife (or daughter or son or second cousin) writes poems too. It's a great hobby, don't you think?"

"Doesn't anyone believe in rhyme anymore?"

"I have this great idea for a poem. All I have to do is write it."

Or my personal favorite, "Would I know your work?"

Another Louis Armstrong question: If they have to ask, nothing you say's gonna help. At this point in the conversation, it's probably best just to shake your head no and try once again to change the subject. At this point, it doesn't really matter whether you've published five well-reviewed books, one recipe in your church newsletter, or nothing at all. Though the questioner probably means well and is only trying to make polite gestures, it's hard after one of these conversations not to feel devalued. A man at a dinner party once suggested that, since no one really reads the kind of things I write, maybe I should write a novel instead. I didn't tell him that I had done just that—that in fact I'd written three and I'd had a great time writing them and one of them was pretty good if I do say so myself, though the other two, well. . . .

I didn't tell him, because what he seemed to be saying wasn't that I should write a novel, but that I should *publish* the kind of novel that lots of people would read, a book that would make oodles of money and/or make me famous.

The man was a nice guy, probably a good husband and father, maybe even someone with a passion for painting or gardening or woodworking or sculpting who pursued his passion privately, intensely, the way I pursue writing.

Even so, I felt it best not to tell him about the novels. When we stand outside a process, when we're on the outside looking in, it's impossible to imagine what goes on inside. The man was on the outside looking in, and, corny as this might sound, my memory of writing the unpublished novels was just too precious to share with him. Only I knew what those years had meant to me. What if he brushed those years aside as if they were so much lint? I wanted to keep the memory of each writing day inside me, the way I keep each unpublished essay and poem, even the most flawed, warm and safe within its folder or box. To those standing outside the process, only writing that gets published and makes the writer famous and/or rich matters. To writers living within the process, every word matters, even if no eyes but our own ever read those words.

Misconception # 6. Writers are smarter, more sensitive, and more creative than other people.
Hmmm. This is a tricky one. Since, for the moment at least, I am the writer and you are the reader, I would very much like for you to believe this. But I have to admit that it just isn't so—in my case and in the cases of most of the writers I've met.

Let's start with the intelligence issue. When you judge intelligence solely by academic criteria, writers don't always fare well. Most writers, so research studies show, were B, not A, students; my academic record bears this out. Maybe this is because writers tend to be more interested in questions than in answers. Granted, it takes a keen mind to ask interesting questions, but this doesn't mean that writers are necessarily more brainy or intellectual than other people.

Perhaps they are simply more curious, less afraid of venturing into unknown areas, and more willing, as Proust said, to "become stupid before the canvas."

As for the claim that writers are more sensitive than other people, while it's true that some writers are sensitive people, the same can be said for nonwriters. Sensitivity is a human trait, not necessarily a writerly one, and it manifests itself in any number of ways that have nothing to do with writing. Perhaps the only area in which writers are more sensitive than other people is in the area of language. Just as musicians are sensitive to sound, painters to color, and sculptors to form, writers are sensitive to words.

When people tell me they're just not creative enough to write, I usually answer, "There is no such thing as a creative person. There is only the created act." This is not my original idea; it comes from Rollo May's *The Courage to Create*. "Creativity," May writes, "is basically the process of making, or bringing into being." As such, "creativity can be seen only in the act."

This theory may get your hackles up. You might argue that this just isn't so, that creative people do indeed exist. You might cite your nephew, who, in your opinion, is one of the most creative people on the planet. "OK," I'd say, "I'll go along with that. But first tell me how you know he's creative. What evidence do you have?" For without evidence of something made, something brought into being, there can be no creation. Even the God of Genesis wasn't creative until he created the heavens and the earth. Your nephew, or mine, isn't creative simply because he daydreams a lot, likes weird movies, or has fluorescent tricolored hair—unless, of course, his hair is his created act, a work of art.

Those of us who aspire to art—writers, painters, sculptors, designers—like to think of ourselves as creative individuals. The truth is, we are creative only because we create.

Even if our creation never comes into the public eye, even if it never reaches completion in terms of what the world considers complete, nevertheless the process of its making—and only that process—makes us creative.

How does one become creative? One *creates*. What freedom exists in that thought, what possibility! Yet, as our parents warned us as they handed over the car keys, along with freedom comes responsibility. If creativity resides only within the process of making, we must toss aside the excuse that we aren't creative enough; we'll have to find a new excuse not to create. But if, on the other hand, we're still basking in the haloed memory of some grandfather or teacher telling us how creative we are, we must ask ourselves what we're waiting for. The playing field's been leveled; we're all chosen for the team.

CHAPTER 2

TIME AND SPACE FOR WRITING

FIND SPACE FOR WRITING

A few years ago, a friend gave me a book of Jill Krementz's portraits of writers in their private working spaces. The photographs appeal to the voyeur in me. I'm hungry for knowledge about how other writers live and work. I like seeing their file cabinets, the coffee cups and cereal boxes stacked beside their typewriters, the views from their windows, their cats sprawled on manuscript pages. Some of the writers hold spiral notebooks or legal pads. Some use manual typewriters. One is dictating into a machine. And some don't seem to be writing at all. They're staring out the window, talking on the phone, working the crossword puzzle, or reading while their works in progress sit patiently waiting.

It's one thing to read a writer's published words; it's quite another to glimpse the human and often chaotic conditions under which these words were written. Photographs, of course, can't tell the whole truth—they're arranged to appeal to the eye. Even so, I'm warmed by the behind-the-scenes stories the photographs suggest. (The barefoot people in pajamas, I imagine, are morning writers like me.) Opening the door to a writer's private space, I'm reminded that however grand our theories about writing, finally it comes down to this: one human being in one place at one time with one particular set of tools, trying to write her heart out.

A room of one's own

Growing up in a household of six children, I had little opportunity to be alone. I shared a bedroom, and usually a bed, with one or more of my sisters or with a great-aunt who lived with our family. Although I usually enjoyed the company, at times I craved a space of my own where I could write songs, stories, and poems. Since the bathroom was the most private space in the house, the bathtub became my study, my dreaming space, my locked diary. It was the "room of one's own" Virginia Woolf wrote of, though I had not yet heard of Woolf, nor did I imagine that my struggle for writing solitude would become a lifelong obsession.

Most writers require at least a degree of solitude; some employ extreme measures to achieve it. They rent motel rooms, borrow an uncle's mountain cabin, migrate from one writers colony to another, leave "Gone writing" notes for their spouses and children, or just generally disappear from view. But most of us must keep one foot planted in the world of job, family, and daily commerce and one foot in the world of writing. A tricky stance, perhaps, but somehow we manage. One of my friends, a college professor and family man, drives to his office early on Saturday mornings and writes. Another friend rents a tiny storage room in the basement of his apartment building.

If you need solitude, you might be able to beg, steal, or borrow to secure a private space outside your home. But if circumstances demand that you write at home, finding solitude may demand some ingenuity. During graduate school when I rented a room from a woman with four children, one of whom slept in the twin bed beside me, I put a folding screen between the beds, placed my typewriter on a TV tray, and sat on my bed to work. Later when I married a man with a son who claimed the spare room, I staked out a corner of the unfinished basement and cleared space on an old Formica table. Plumbing pipes snaked above my head, and the ancient oil furnace groaned and rumbled beside me, but I was ecstatic. A writing room of my own: What more could I possibly need?

Though I have since trained myself to write almost anywhere—trains, planes, libraries, coffee shops, dentist offices—and with any number of people surrounding me, at heart I am still the child in the bathtub. Most days, I prefer to write in a quiet, private place with as few distractions as possible. As I write these words I'm at my desk in my apartment in New York City, facing the wall rather than the window (there's too much to see out there, too many places for my eyes to travel), and though the phone is ringing, I'm not answering it. I've plugged my ears with tiny rubber sponges and tuned the white noise machine to "ocean," and with each crash of a wave, I dive a little deeper. If I'm lucky, within a few minutes I won't be here, but *there*, submerged in the dark, quiet place where writing dwells.

Alternatives to the desk
Though Krementz's book of photographs is titled *The Writer's Desk*, many of her subjects aren't stationed at desks at all. They're lying in beds, sitting at kitchen tables, reclining on chairs or sofas. One stands at a drafting table; one paces the floor; another is perched on the top of a kitchen counter, a portable computer in her lap.

A desk is only one place for writing to occur. Robert Bly wrote all his poems for *Morning Poems* in bed, one poem per morning. He woke early and stayed in bed until the day's poem was drafted. Though your schedule might not allow for this kind of freedom, you might try writing in bed for at least a few minutes as part of your morning or nighttime ritual. Since beds are intimate places, bed writing encourages private sharing, secrets and whispers, a kind of pillow talk for the page. Beds can also bring out our sensual and sexual natures, which might be too shy to reveal themselves at the desk. And because beds are usually safe, secure places, even our ill, wounded, or half-dressed selves can feel at home there and settle down comfortably among the covers. If we're too sleepy to censor ourselves or judge the words flowing from our pen, well, maybe that's OK. Maybe, like the milk toast and cocoa our mothers served us, a little writing in bed is just what the doctor ordered.

Any space where you put pen to paper, hand to keyboard, voice to recorder—or simply sit and dream your way into words—can be a writing space. I like having several alternatives to suit my writing tasks. The bed is for early morning journal writing, the desk is where I draft poems and essays in longhand, the computer station is for typing up handwritten drafts, and the card table is where I make major structural changes in long pieces, a process that often entails physically cutting and pasting sections before they go back to the desk for further revision or to the computer for final editing.

James Dickey kept several typewriters in various locations throughout his house, and as he roamed from room to room, he typed a line here, an image there. Consider setting up various writing "stages" throughout your house or work space and moving among them. You don't have to write for long periods of time. Plant slips of paper in books so you can record ideas that occur to you while you're reading; keep scissors and self-stick pads near newspapers and magazines; put note cards in the kitchen, the living room, the bathroom. Then, every week or so, gather up your ideas and record them in your journal or file them for future use.

Public spaces

Many years ago when my three-year-old niece Sarah was spending the weekend with my husband and me, another couple dropped by for drinks and conversation. As the evening grew late, I took Sarah upstairs to bed, kissed her and her doll good night, and closed the door. A few hours later she appeared at the bottom of the stairs, rubbing her eyes and grasping the doll by its matted hair. "We can't sleep in all that quiet," she said.

Sarah ended up falling asleep—quite easily, I recall—on the sofa beside me. The lights were on, the stereo was playing, the grown-ups were laughing, and she slept through it all. Watching her, I recalled the childhood comfort of falling asleep in the midst of noisy activity. At my grandparents' house, the ambient sounds lulled me—the clink of glasses, the crack of peanut shells, the deep-throated laughter of my uncles, the shuffle and slap of euchre cards. Sleep was a dark and silent place to enter alone, but surrounded by voices and light, I fell softly, effortlessly, into it.

Writing, like sleep, can be a lonely space to enter, and at times even those of us who crave solitude and silence may feel that we just can't write in all that quiet. The bubble of privacy we've created draws too much attention to itself. Suddenly every noise is amplified; we are conscious of our own unsteady breathing, the blood thrumming in our ears. The silence is, as the cliché goes, deafening, the auditory equivalent of a blank page. The pressure builds. Why can't I think of anything to write? Why can't I finish this sentence? If the anxiety continues, we may start watching ourselves write—or worse, not write.

On days when even the simplest words seem to have gone into hiding, I grab my notebook and head out the door. At the park, ducks are squawking, Frisbees whizzing, in-line skates whirring—a cosmic noise machine. Sometimes I let the sounds wash over me until they recede into the background; sometimes I tune in particular stations. I record scraps of conversation, eavesdrop on arguments, and try to guess the dramas beneath: "No," says the woman in the green coat as she walks beside the bearded man. "I've said it before, and I'll say it again. I can only serve one master."

The first line of a story? Perhaps. If I'm between writing projects, my park jottings often trigger new poems, stories, or essays. And if I'm stalled in the middle of a project, the force of a random sight or sound sometimes loosens the inner hinges and gets me moving again. Maybe I've been too narrowly focused, too locked into one notion of what the piece should be or say. Art is partly what happens in the space between opposing notions; inner collides with outer, private with public, and this collision brings something new into being. At the park I listen and watch. If I'm lucky, the mottled duck on the bank will waddle out of its marshy context and into my essay, or one of the lines in my troubled poem will break free and sail toward the branch of the ginkgo tree.

Even on park days when nothing gets written, the act of getting outside helps me get outside myself, that hermetically sealed space where writing too often takes me. Things slide into their proper places; I regain perspective. The world won't stop, I remind myself, if my ragged couplet doesn't find its rhyme. And no one ever died from a faulty line break. Watching the outdoor parade—the bald man walking his dachshund, the teenage couple with their thumbs hooked in each other's belt loops, the gray-haired woman pushing twins in a stroller—I remember I'm part of the parade too.

There's a warm animal comfort in being surrounded by others while your mind is off on its solitary pursuits. Writing in a public place allows you to keep one foot in the physical world and one in the world of imagination, a stance that's hard to maintain at home. Loved ones require your whole attention, body and soul—as you require theirs. But here among strangers, your mind is free to come and go as it pleases. The boy beside you on the park bench probably won't ask for help with his homework; the waitress at the coffee shop won't ask what you're making for dinner. Anonymity grants invisibility, which means that public places often provide more writing privacy than do our own homes. In the park, the cafe, or the hotel lobby, your doorbell won't chime, your soup won't boil over, and—unless you carry a mobile—the phone solicitors won't find you.

Even if you don't consciously seek out public writing spaces, chances are you spend more time in public places than you do at your desk anyway. So why not enroll in what I call the "Paladin School of Writing," named for the character in the fifties television show *Have Gun Will Travel*. Have pen, will travel. Carry paper in your purse, pocket, or gym bag. Keep a notebook in your glove compartment for those times when you're stalled in traffic, or plant a cassette recorder on the front seat for taping ideas while you're driving. As I mentioned earlier, sitting at a desk is only one way to write, and if you sit too long in one place, you may get stiff, psychologically as well as physically. At a certain point in the writing process, moving around is good not only for your muscles and joints but also for your mind. So go ahead. Pace the floor, stretch, stand, go for a swim, or jog until the words start flowing again.

MAKE TIME FOR WRITING

As I've said before, writing only happens by writing. There is simply no way around it: You must make time for writing to occur. Some people don't like the idea of scheduling writing. It's like trying to schedule sex, one friend told me. He says he writes only when he feels inspired or when the mood hits him. If, like my friend, you chafe at the idea of making and keeping a writing schedule, then it may be that inspiration itself is your schedule, the only appointment you are committed to keeping.

One challenge in keeping a writing schedule based only on inspiration is that in order for writing to occur, you must be able to drop everything at a moment's notice and attend to the task the muse sets before you. This can be hard to do if you also have children, a full-time job, or other commitments that cannot be easily abandoned. Working solely on inspiration's schedule may also preclude writing the kind of sustained piece that requires multiple revisions, outside research, or a lengthy incubation period. And finally, as I mentioned before, waiting for inspiration to magically appear and nudge you toward some writing task might mean that you wait a long, long time, possibly forever—and possibly at the wrong door. Maybe inspiration isn't hiding, as you'd always imagined, in some golden-edged sunset or foam-capped wave. Maybe, even as you read these words, the muse is arranging herself seductively between two keys of your typewriter or computer, just waiting for you to make the first move.

If you're one of those writers whose writing gets accomplished solely on inspiration's schedule, consider yourself lucky—and highly unusual. For the rest of us, making time for writing usually means just that: *making* time. If your experience is anything like mine, you'll probably find that time doesn't come to you. You have to go to it. This may require stalking time, stealing time, or simply taking it, by force if necessary.

Your writing schedule
If the idea of a writing schedule is new to you, try easing yourself into it the way you would ease yourself into a diet or exercise regime. If you don't, you're likely to become discouraged after the first flush of excitement wears off. Here are some questions to consider before you commit to a particular writing schedule:

What is the best time of day for me to write?
A workable writing schedule takes into consideration, among other things, your life circumstances and the

rhythm of your days. If you're a night owl who must get up early to shower, dress, make breakfast and pack lunches for three children, drop them off at school, then drive thirty minutes to your job in the city, you might consider writing late at night or on Sunday evenings when the kids are visiting your parents. But if you're a morning person, you might consider writing early in the morning, before anyone else in your household is awake.

Writing takes energy, so you also need to consider what time of day or night you feel most energetic and focused. If you write only when you're exhausted or distracted, or only in leftover moments between crises, both you and your writing will suffer. Try to save a portion of your best time for writing.

During the years I taught high school English, making time to write was a challenge. Since I had to arrive at school before 7:00 A.M. and was too exhausted to write at the end of the school day, my only workable option turned out to be early morning writing—and I do mean early. For several years I rose at 4:30 and wrote until 6:00. The first few weeks were difficult; I was groggy and fuzzy headed. But I soon became accustomed to the dark hours when nothing but the words were stirring. When friends found out about my schedule, they made noises about my dedication. "Nonsense," I told them, and I meant it. For me, writing has always been a totally selfish act. When I'm not writing, I'm frustrated and surly. Because the 4:30 appointment was something I made for myself, it was easy to keep—most mornings, anyway.

Before you make drastic changes to accommodate your writing, take a look at the schedule that's already in place. What windows in your schedule open naturally? If no windows open by themselves, which ones can you open? Look closely. Decide which obligations are essential to your well-being and the well-being of your loved ones, let the nonessential go, and reclaim the salvaged time for writing.

How long should my writing sessions be?
Writers vary dramatically on this question. Some prefer brief writing appointments, while others produce their best work during long, caffeine-infused sessions. When scheduling your writing, you need to consider, among other things, your energy level. If your energy level is low, you might require frequent rest breaks; if your energy level is high, you might prefer to push yourself or, as Annie Dillard suggests, to "write till you drop."

Also, consider your natural work style. Do you ease your way slowly into a task, carrying ideas in your head and reconsidering them as you go about your daily business? Or do you use the blank page as your canvas, later cutting and pasting your way to a finished product? For writers who mentally draft and revise, much work has already been done by the time they sit down at their desks, so their writing sessions might not need to be long to be effective. On the other hand, a multiple-draft writer often requires longer periods of desk time before she finds her way into and out of a piece.

Your writing task also affects the length of your writing sessions. If you're writing in your journal—to clear your mind, record an experience, or just have fun with words—fifteen minutes a day might be plenty of time. But if you're drafting a long piece, you may need several sustained hours. Whatever your goal, you need to allow time to enter the writing totally, not just skim the surface. And once you're immersed in the writing, you need time to think, reflect, experiment, play, make mistakes, and if necessary, start again. Some writers, especially those who submerge themselves in fictional worlds where characters and places become more real than the world at their elbow, may also require depressurization time in which they resurface slowly so as not to suffer from the psychological equivalent of the bends.

But don't be discouraged if you can't make a lot of time for writing. You'll be surprised at how much you can accomplish in short sessions. Jill McCorkle wrote her first novel in one-page increments: a page each morning before she left for her job as a librarian. In some cases, time limitations can actually work to your advantage, freeing you from censoring, judging, or condemning the work in progress. If your writing time is necessarily brief, it is also precious, so why waste any of it worrying about what you're not able to do or what you're doing poorly? There's no time for such matters. There's time only to apply pen to paper; the devil take the rest.

Time limits may also force you to write in more original ways than you might if you had too much time on your hands. A busy writer is like the young couple furnishing their first apartment with garage sale items and hand-me-downs. Sure, the affluent family down the block may have a houseful of new furniture, but chances are the look is a yawn: Everything matches and nothing feels earned. But the young couple's place? Well, who would have thought the nail barrel would make such a great end table, the bedspread such a stunning tablecloth? Necessity is a mother, and invention is her brightest child.

It's often said that if you need something accomplished, give the task to a busy person. Busy people know how to budget time and juggle multiple tasks. Since they don't have time to leisurely consider and reconsider every option, they don't stop to consider. They *act*. Meanwhile, the person with too much time on his hands paces in the corner of the room, hesitant as Hamlet. His novel may never get written.

How often should I write?
Scheduling writing into your life doesn't mean that you must write every day. Some writers work one or two afternoons a week, on weekends, only while traveling, or only in the summer when they're not teaching classes. Edmund White says he can go a year or two without picking up his pen.

In his essay "The Writer as Student and Teacher," David Huddle suggests that you write often enough so that you miss it if you don't do it. "To have a real writing life," he says, "you must be writing at least this often." I agree. If you wait too long between sessions, you may have to spend valuable writing time trying to get reacquainted with the process.

Also, particularly if you're working on a long project such as a novel or a literary essay, you might find that you lose momentum or interest if too much time elapses between writing appointments. Early on in the drafting process, it's probably best to space your writing sessions as close together as possible to sustain not only your excitement for the piece but also a consistent mood, tone, and voice. Later on, more widely spaced writing sessions may allow the work to "cool," which will help you achieve the editorial distance you need for the revision process.

Finally, the essential issue isn't when you write, how long, or even how often, but rather the serious commitment you make to writing, a commitment you honor by scheduling writing into your life and then keeping the appointments.

When push comes to shove
If you can't seem to make time for writing, or if you have trouble staying at the desk once you've made the time, first ask yourself why. It could be that you're crippled by some of the misconceptions I mentioned in the first chapter. Ex-

amining the source of your difficulties may help you establish a workable writing schedule or help get you back on course if you've veered off.

But sometimes this very act of examination becomes a way to avoid doing your heart's work. At this point, it's usually best to stop worrying about why you're not writing and to simply sit down and write. Here are some suggestions that have worked for me when all I really needed was to get myself to the desk and stay there:

1. Lower your standards. Rather than saying "I'm going to write a beautiful poem about my month in Paris," say "I'm going to write a poem." Period. Then write it.

2. Think quantity, not quality. Set a timer and write until it goes off, or decide on a set number of words or pages per session, and don't get up from the desk until you're finished. (Anthony Trollope wrote seven pages a day, forty-nine pages a week, sticking so closely to this schedule that if he finished a novel on his fourth page of a day's work, he started the next novel on his fifth page.)

3. Be your own writing instructor. Give yourself writing assignments, then do them.

4. Hold yourself hostage at the desk. Don't comb your hair. Dress in such shabby clothes that you wouldn't dare answer the door or go out for a paper. Then stay at the desk until you've accomplished your task.

5. Set short-term rewards for yourself. Draft six pages = a cookie. Write two hours = a walk in the park. Finish chapter three = a new hat.

6. When your writing is really cooking, don't stop until it's done, no matter how long it takes.

Or:

When your writing is really cooking, make yourself stop. Stop at the most exciting point, when you know exactly what will happen next. Stop in the middle of a phrase if you have to. Then you won't have to start from scratch on your next writing day; you can continue on the high point at which you exited.

7. Eliminate the fear of the empty page by writing a few opening lines the night before a writing session.

8. Right before you go to bed, reread the last thing you wrote. Write a brief response or jot down questions the writing hasn't yet answered. Who knows? You might dream the answers.

9. If all else fails, write down all the reasons why you can't write. Go ahead, get it out of your system. At the end of the session, you may discover that it takes more energy to avoid writing than it does to write. At any rate, you'll have filled some pages, a task you were convinced you couldn't do.

CHAPTER 3

PRIVATE WRITING

When you write for your eyes only, you lock the door and enter alone. No one is watching, judging, assigning. You are free to write anything you want in any way you want. You don't have to finish what you start; you don't have to shape your writing for other eyes to see. Private writing can take many shapes, including journals, dream records, unsent letters, bits of dialogue, drafts of poems or stories, confessions, rants, or any form you choose. And if your writing feels formless, that's OK too. Behind the locked door there are no rules to follow or break. Private writing is just that: private. Think of it as your personal heartbeat.

This doesn't mean you have to write about yourself or only about personal concerns; private writing can just as easily be about public ideas, events, or issues. You may even choose to share your private writing. Since it belongs only to you, how you use it is your business. There are as many uses for private writing as there are writers. For some, it serves as a catharsis, a way to relieve emotional tension and pain. For others, it's a way to record events, trace life passages, and order experiences. Some even use private writing to explore ideas and images which later develop into literary pieces. In this chapter, we'll review some of the more traditional approaches to private writing, such as diaries and journals (terms that I'll use interchangeably), while also exploring alternative approaches.

THE INTIMATE JOURNAL
Though we usually think of diaries as private records, many diaries are written as if an imagined other is listening in. "Dear Kitty," begins Anne Frank's diary, "I hope I will be

able to confide everything to you, as I have never been able to confide in anyone, and I hope you will be a great source of comfort and support." Even if you don't address your diary or journal by name, when you commit your personal thoughts to the page, you are in effect constructing another self with whom you share intimate confidences. The phrases associated with private writing suggest this intimacy: When we *make an entry* in a diary or journal, we enter it as we might enter a secret room, a guarded conversation, or a lover's bed; *keeping a journal* is not only an act of care and guardianship but also one of personal possession. We are possessive of our innermost thoughts. We don't want just anyone listening in.

Not that we don't have friends, spouses, lovers, therapists, priests, or pets in whom to confide. (My cat is one of the best listeners I know.) But there is nothing like the intimacy that occurs within diary pages. The page never yawns, interrupts, or walks away with its tail in the air. It just listens.

Sometimes we whisper secrets. The diary leans close and attends to each word. It will never betray our confidence. Its lips are sealed.

Sometimes we rant and rave, flail and pound against the journal's pages; we curse our lives and everyone in them. The journal is our punching bag, our padded cell. It absorbs the blows.

Sometimes we confess. We enter the booth, and the journal lifts the partition. It is more forgiving than any father-confessor. No matter that it's been three weeks or three years since our last confession. The journal welcomes us home.

When we whine like a spoiled brat, the diary simply leans back, folds its arms across its chest, and nods. It doesn't send us to our room; it doesn't tell us to stop acting like a child.

And when we make no sense, when one phrase tangles in the next and we can't untie the knot, the journal is patient. It's not going anywhere. It's got all the time in the world. Besides, a journal knows our history as well as we do, sometimes even better. Because it has recorded each confidence, it can recall our past and, in so doing, help us imagine the future. This too will pass, it seems to say. Like a longtime partner who knows us well enough to finish our sentences or fill in the blanks when we're searching for a word, a journal can fill the awkward silences. When we are voiceless, it helps us find our voice again.

Sometimes the voice we find is strange or otherworldly, singing in an unknown key. We dream dreams and see visions. Our daylight self tells us these dreams are crazy, impractical, impossible to achieve, so why even bother? The diary says, "Tell me more." When we do, wc can be assured our visions are stored safely away. Like the dream keeper Langston Hughes writes of in his poem "The Dream Keeper," the diary wraps our "heart melodies" in a "blue cloud cloth, away from the too rough fingers of the world."

PRIVATE WRITING AS A PLAYROOM

The world outside our door is not only rough, it can also be deadly serious. Grown-ups are expected to act in a grown-up fashion. We are supposed to pay our bills, mow our lawns, go to our jobs, keep our checkbooks balanced. Even writing, which might have begun as a delightful leisure activity, a playful way to pass the hours, can become burdened with grown-up expectations. Without intending to, we carry our nose-to-the-grindstone notions into our writing rooms. We tell ourselves we must write about important issues and not waste our time in frivolity. Our journals must be tools for self-improvement; they must teach us something. No more doodling in the margins, no more Saturday afternoons making up poems about three-toed tree toads.

When I lose the simple joy of writing for writing's sake, which happens more often than I care to admit, it's usually because I've been viewing my writing as a task that must be accomplished. It's easy to see how this can happen when one is writing on assignment or under a publisher's deadline. But journal writing? How in the world did that become a chore?

When this happens, I force myself to take three giant steps backward to survey the situation. Private writing, I remind myself, is for my eyes only. No one is looking over my shoulder. There's no one to please. So why the pursed lips, the furrowed brow? If there is no joy in Mudville, why keep stepping up to the plate?

Thinking of writing as child's play is the best way I know to find my way happily back to the page. Kids aren't afraid to be silly, so when I want to play in my journal I start by recording all the silly thoughts and goofy ideas that occur to me: "The man's wife was so loose he even caught her in bed with the flu." "Embroidery is crewel and unusual punishment." "Nature isn't the only mother who abhors a vacuum." Sometimes I draw cartoons. In one, a nursing baby is singing, "Thanks for the mammaries." In another, a man is wearing not a checkered past but a plaid one.

I know, I know. They're not that funny. I should definitely keep my day job. But such silliness keeps me amused, and there are times when amusement is what I need from my writing. Who knows, maybe someday I'll write a story about a character who goes around saying goofy things. Stranger things have happened. One of my cartoons—of a dime walking disdainfully past a penny lying in the gutter—evolved into a poem about the invention of zero. You just never know.

Besides silliness, another trait most children share is delight in the sounds and rhythms of musical words and phrases, even when those words carry little or no meaning. "Say it again," my nephew begs. So I bring Lewis Carroll's poem "Jabberwocky" out of mothballs yet once more: " 'Twas brillig, and the slithy toves/Did gyre and gimble in the wabe." Then, primed for fun, I return to the writing desk and begin making lists of wonderful sounding words, the kind of words that, as one of my young students described it, "feel good to my ears": *blub, lurk, aubergine, Nefertiti.* Many writers keep word lists or play with word combinations as they write. "I found these words and put them together by their appetites and respect for each other," wrote poet William Stafford. And Roy Blount Jr.'s published journals contain fascinating sets of word pairs: *lacy pants/participants, baseline/Vaseline, wrapper/reappear.*

I start playing with the word lists, searching for family likenesses: *confetti, graffiti, cherry tree.* If I keep playing long enough, the skeleton of a poem might emerge:

> From the cherry tree,
> blossoms scatter
> like confetti
> onto the curb,
> against the graffiti.

Sometimes I uncover words hidden within other words. I recently discovered *marriage* tucked inside *miscarriage*—an odd discovery that started me thinking "first comes love, then comes marriage, then carriage, miscarriage, miscarriage of justice, justice of the peace." This form of play is like a game of leapfrog; the mind hops from one image to another, one idea to another. Even if the game leads nowhere (there's that serious adult butting in again, suggesting that games are supposed to lead somewhere, produce something!), we've given our minds some healthy exercise and had a little fun along the way.

Thinking of writing as a playroom rather than as a work-room is one of many ways to discover, or rediscover, the joy of private writing. A playroom has no boundaries. Now it's a submarine taking you under. Now it's a forest, dark and unexplored, where exotic creatures lurk. Now it's a trunk filled with dress-up clothes. Now it's the door to an unwritten story for which you have the only key, and, won-der of wonders, the key fits.

A RECORD OF EVENTS

Both *diary* and *journal* are rooted in the Latin word meaning "day," and the first diaries were day-by-day renderings of events and transactions. Clerks documented court proceed-ings, sailors updated logbooks, private citizens recorded their daily comings and goings. Though many writers don't keep journals, those who do seem wedded to the process. William Saroyan, who kept a diary for many years, noted that the journal keeper "is obsessed by the wish to know what happened, and the only way he can ever hope to know is to have the written daily account to consult at his convenience. Otherwise it is all forgotten."

Saroyan's statement may appear old-fashioned, even stodgy, to those who view the journal primarily as a tool for expressing emotions. "Why spend time recording the mundane details of my life?" you might ask. "Aren't there deeper ways to approach writing from the heart?" Though it might appear that a journal rooted in day-by-day detail precludes exploration of your deepest joys, desires, and fears, in some cases a journal based on external events can actually reveal your inner life more than a journal in which only raw emotions are recorded.

One reason for this is that we tend to write in emotion-based journals only when we're sad, angry, or otherwise upset. Not only can this be embarrassing to us later, but it also gives a false impression of our lives. Where are the lustrous, dazzling moments when, to paraphrase Wordsworth, our hearts leapt up? Most likely, during these times we were too busy being happy to stop and record the happiness.

Another reason why emotion-based journals sometimes mask our deepest selves rather than reveal them is that when we record our emotions, we tend to speak in generalities and abstractions: "I'm so sad today, I feel as though my world has ended." "I screamed until my throat was raw, but I still felt angry." Though the writing of such passages might momentarily relieve our stress, they won't help us retrace the emotional terrain of our lives because the pebbles, shrubs, and soil of the terrain are missing. Words like *sad, jealous*, and *upset* are labels; they tell rather than show. When you use such labels, you skip over the physical details that might help you reenter the experience that evoked the emotion. But if, on the other hand, you describe the particular event or image that triggered these emotions— the fresh tattoo zigzagging across your son's arm, the click and whir of the respirator beside your father's hospital bed, the rosy shimmer of the stockings on the woman who crossed her legs seductively when your husband entered the room—you might be better able to reenter these emotions if and when you choose to.

Though daily accounts of what happened don't appeal to everyone, the benefits of keeping such accounts are many. First, as Saroyan mentions, a journal helps jog our memories of past events, the places and people we have known. Second, a journal encourages regular appointments with the desk and provides an orderly place to store the chaotic pieces of our lives. Third, journal keeping prompts us to notice the extraordinary detail in even the most ordinary day.

And finally, if we later choose to share our journals, or if our descendants choose to, the journals will serve as records of particular places and times. When we read the diaries of Samuel Pepys, Fanny Burney, or Sei Shonagon, we're treated to a cultural and historical education more lively than any textbook account. Even the most casual, nonliterary record can open windows into personal and public histories. My grandmother kept a shorthand diary by jotting notes on her kitchen calendar: "butter and cream for Sisson's," "three chicks pipped today," "macaroni for Grange supper." Her sister, Great-Aunt Bessie, kept more detailed observations of daily events—trips taken, books read, rare birds sighted, and the external and internal weather of her days. Reading her diaries, I learn from the inside out how it felt to be a teenager in the Gay Nineties, a farmer and Red Cross volunteer during World War I, and a widow who traveled the country by Greyhound bus during the fifties: "I've soaked my corns in both the Atlantic and the Pacific," she wrote.

A diary rooted in daily detail is a double gift to its reader. When we read someone else's diary or reread our own, we learn not only about the person who recorded these particular details but also about the world in which the author moved. "No man is an island," wrote John Donne; no woman is either. We breathe and move on a continent larger than any one self, and the landscape of that continent shapes us. The stories of our lives are also the stories of the towns we've visited, the people we've known, the books we've read, the clothes we've bought, the vaccinations we've received, the cats and dogs we've named and buried, the meals we've prepared and eaten. Keeping a record of our comings and goings reminds us that our lives are continuing sagas unfolding, in specific detail, day after particular day.

REWRITING THE CALENDAR
One of the pleasures of private writing is discovering the internal rhythms, chapters, passages, and calendars of our

lives. I applaud the discipline of those who keep daily records of life events, especially those who are able to fit these records into tidy calendar-dated books. Holding one of these books, I imagine a life so orderly and well paced that something pageworthy occurs each day, but nothing so pageworthy as to spill over into the next day's space. Each day is equally important, say these diaries, and each year of a person's life begins on January 1 and ends on December 31. My reverence for such order is deeply ingrained. When I received my first diary on my tenth birthday, I forced myself to wait four months, until January 1, to start writing in it.

Over the next years I started three or four of these diaries, and a pattern soon developed. January began with a bang—intricate details of the Rose Parade and our neighbors' black-eyed pea suppers, followed by my New Year's resolutions, chief of which was to fill each of my diary's pages. But by February I was wearing down, and not even the thrill of my first date with Jimmer Cunningham could find its way into the diary's pages. Nothing had happened to me for weeks, and now this! How could I possibly contain all I had to say on one page?

Try as I might, I couldn't force the realities of my real, messy life to fit into preassigned slots, and I was about to give up when I discovered a rack of unlined, undated journals at the stationery store. Spiral notebooks or legal pads would have allowed me the same freedom, but they lacked the aesthetic and psychological appeal of a journal. I liked how one felt in my hands. I liked its smooth white pages. And because it was a book, the pages bound between two sturdy covers, I felt like an author. The book I was writing was the book of my life, a life that didn't follow the one-page-a-day, January-through-December metronome beat but rather was improvised experience by experience, thought by thought, emotion by emotion. I no longer had to pad an entry with meaningless words simply for the sake of filling a page, nor did I have to restrain myself from writing as much as I wanted on those days when words seized me.

THE PASSAGE JOURNAL

One alternative to the calendar-based journal is what I call the passage journal. In a passage journal, you record your journey not through a particular week, month, or year, but through a particular life passage. The passage may be fearful or joyful, planned or unexpected, seemingly trivial or potentially life altering, time restricted or ongoing. Maybe you're training for a marathon, learning a new language, starting Lamaze classes, going away to college, or planning a wedding. You might be facing a difficult task—selling the family farm, starting a round of chemotherapy, preparing to leave a failed marriage or career. Or the passage might be based not on external events but rather on some internal journey—tracing your relationship with your father, say, or writing your way toward a crucial decision.

The passage you record doesn't have to be a painful one, nor does it have to be one that seems, at first glance, especially significant. I kept one passage journal during a month's trip to England; another, while I was teaching an experimental writing class at an inner-city high school. Any journey, inner or outer, can be material for a passage journal, and sometimes the seemingly trivial events yield more surprises than those events that loom large.

If you know in advance that you'll be embarking on a new passage, try to begin your entries early in the process. But if an unexpected event triggers your passage, such as the death of a loved one or the loss of a job, you probably won't be able to start the journal immediately. Begin whenever you feel the time is right. My friend started a journal one month after an automobile accident claimed her daughter's life. The journal I kept during the period my husband and I were separated was begun three weeks after he moved out. Because I had no idea how long the separation might last—"perhaps forever," I would write at one point—I wasn't sure how large a journal I would need. But I knew I needed a book devoted solely to the events, thoughts, dreams, and emotions directly related to the separation. The physicality of the process (buying the book, opening its cover, counting the blank pages, watching the pages fill with words as the months went by) reminded me that I was living a story that had a beginning and a middle and would one day have an end, even if it wasn't the end I hoped for.

As it turned out, the separation lasted six months; the journal, ten. Four months after the reconciliation, I closed the cover on that particular story, and for many years I didn't reread the journal. Even now, more than a decade since the separation, some of the entries are painful to reenter. Still, I am grateful I kept the journal. During a painful time, it offered solace and order; now it serves as a record. Rereading it, I am reminded that however chaotic our experiences may appear on the surface, there is a story line threaded beneath them.

Though most passage journals are written in the midst of an event or experience, others are written months or even years after the external passage is completed. In this kind of journal, the external passage (the months of chemotherapy, the trip to Europe, the birth of your child) serves as the trigger for the internal journey that is only now beginning in the journal keeper's mind. In *Holy the Firm*, Annie Dillard says, "There are no events but thoughts and the heart's hard turning, the heart's slow learning where to love and whom." When you start a passage journal after the external event is over, the reflection itself becomes the event, the passage through which you are moving.

Seen this way, the journal that reflects on the past is a present record, but rather than focusing on details of the experience as it's occurring, it focuses on present-tense thoughts, memories, and emotions regarding the past experience. Geneviève Jurgensen's *The Disappearance* is an example of this kind of journal. She began writing it twelve years after the journal's triggering event: the accidental deaths of her two young daughters. Since Jurgensen's journal is a reflection, it follows not the chronology of the events surrounding the deaths but rather the chronology of Jurgensen's memory journey through these events.

Whichever type of journal you choose to keep—a record of a passage as it's occurring or a record of your internal journey to understand the completed event—the writing process is the same. Begin your first entry as soon as you feel the need to record, then write often and deeply, and continue writing in the journal until the passage reaches a natural end or you no longer feel the need to write. Either way, you will have recorded one of the stories of your life— a story with a beginning, middle, and end, even if the end seems to have no firm ending and the passage is one you must keep negotiating and renegotiating.

PRIVATE WRITING AS TRUTH TELLING

On my tenth birthday, Great-Aunt Bessie gave me a small pink vinyl-covered diary with a tiny lock and key. Before this time, I'd never thought of words as secrets I could lock away. The newfound power was exhilarating. If I had the only key, no one else could read what I'd written—not my parents, teachers, siblings, or friends. I could write whatever I wanted, bad words too, and no one would know. I could scribble, misspell words right and left, even tell lies without getting caught.

Not that I wanted to lie. What I wanted was to tell what the witnesses on *Perry Mason* promised to tell: the whole truth and nothing but. The whole truth, I'd discovered, was hard to say to other people. Sometimes their feelings got hurt, or they scowled in disappointment, or worse, they laughed at me and walked away. "If you can't say something nice, don't say anything at all," my third-grade teacher had admonished. That kept me quiet for years. If a friend asked what I thought of her new pixie haircut, I complimented her, no matter what; if another friend asked if she looked fat in the yellow tent dress, I shook my head no. Politeness, kindness, cowardice, call it what you will. The result was the same: white lie upon white lie upon white lie. A snow-covered field of untruths.

Little white lies hurt no one, we say. It's the big lies that count. The problem with little white lies is that we can get so used to saying what we think we're supposed to say— the safe, expedient, rational, correct thing—that we forget how to say what we truly feel. And if we can't say what we feel, we can't write our hearts out. Private writing offers us the chance to *consciously tell the truth*. This phrase comes from my friend Peter White, who distinguishes conscious truth telling from the everyday brand of truth telling that most of us practice. In the everyday brand, though we may essentially be telling the truth—that is, we're not voicing any falsehoods—we're telling the truth not for its own sake but rather to suit a particular situation or to advance our own causes. To consciously tell the truth, on the other hand, is to say what is true solely for the sake of saying what is true, rather than as part of some other agenda.

When we try, through writing, to consciously tell the truth, we may discover new truths or find our way back to truths we've lost. I lose my way so often that I've devised rituals for finding my way back. When I'm feeling exceptionally bold, I take the direct approach suggested by these lines from Muriel Rukeyser:

What would happen if one woman told the truth
   about herself?
The world would split open.

OK, I ask, what am I afraid to say about myself? The last
thing I want to do is to split my safe, orderly world open,
but if I can't tell the truth about myself, how can I expect
to tell the truth about anything or anyone else? I pick up
the pen and begin, "The truth is," and I write whatever
comes to mind as quickly as I can, before I lose my nerve.
"The truth is I envy C's life. I'm afraid to say that I'm lonely.
The truth is I'm getting old, my eyelids are drooping, my
poems are. . . ."

As I write, I allow contradictions, dichotomies, and illog-
ical statements to come forth, for truth almost always has
more than one side. "I love New York and hate New York."
"The old woman's breasts were shrunken and beautiful."
"Money is the most stupid and important thing in our
lives." "I wanted to kiss him and never see him again."

When I've finished writing everything that comes to
mind, contradictions and all, I address the second line of
Rukeyser's quotation. What world would split open if I
told the truth? Would my husband leave me, my publisher
cancel my contract, my parents disown me, my friends lose
their respect for me? I write furiously, nonstop, about the
worst that could possibly happen. Then I take a deep breath
and read what I've written. What a relief. None of these
terrible things need happen, I tell myself, because this writing need never leave this room. If I want, I can shred the
pages or burn them in the fireplace.

Even if I were to make the hardest truths public, chances
are the worst probably wouldn't happen. But if I persist in
thinking that it would, I remind myself that these words
are for my eyes only. If I tell the whole truth and nothing
but, the worst that can happen—which almost always turns

out to be the best that can happen—is that my inner world might split open, shattering old notions, white lies, and misconceptions.

On days when I'm feeling frightened or vulnerable, when I'm unable to speak the truth no matter how hard I try, I take the indirect approach. "Give a man a mask," wrote Oscar Wilde, "and he will tell you the truth." The mask I assume may be a story, game, traditional poetry form, or any writing activity that deflects my mind from the head-on task of truth telling. After all, there are consequences for telling the truth, even if you're the only listener, and who of us is always eager to pay such consequences? To trick myself into truth telling, I sometimes borrow an idea from my writing playground, one of any number of exercises I keep on hand to jump-start the writing process. Later, reading over what I've written, I often find that I've told the truth in spite of myself.

USING PRIVATE WRITING TO LOCATE YOUR TRUE SUBJECTS

One of the problems with being a student who is "good with words" is that you may learn early on how to be glib, how to say what the teacher wants to hear in five hundred words or less and get a decent grade for it. If you were one of those students, as I was, you may be lucky enough to meet along the way a teacher or editor who calls your bluff, insisting that you find an honest way into and out of a subject of your own choosing. Or, on a momentous birthday—forty, fifty, sixty—you may suddenly realize that life is too short to waste any of it writing from someone else's passions rather than from your own.

I'm not suggesting you can't discover passion for a subject that's suggested or assigned by someone else. Like an arranged marriage that unexpectedly develops into a steamy coupling, writing that begins mildly, at an intellectual or emotional distance, sometimes grows into heartfelt writing. But when you have the freedom to write anything you want, why not begin with what matters most to you? Assuming, of course, that you know what matters most. It took me years to set aside notions of what I *should* be writing (meaning someone else's assignment) and attend to what Samuel Butler called "what refuses to go away."

One way to locate your most urgent subjects is to ask yourself, "Where is my heart breaking?" or "What breaks my heart?" Make a list of the fears and concerns that keep you awake at night and interfere with your days. Think of your list as a rosary you finger one bead at a time. Rather than including large, sweeping topics (world hunger, abortion, nuclear disarmament, the disintegration of the family), name specific people, problems, fears, and issues. "I'm afraid my mother will die in a nursing home." "I'm worried that my daughter's husband is having an affair." "How will I make ends meet when I retire?" "What if the biopsy is positive?" Even if you later choose not to write about your own experiences, listing your personal heartbreaks will help you locate public issues for which you feel a strong passion, commitment, or interest. Your concern about your mother, for instance, might lead to an examination of nursing home conditions; your fear of developing cancer might prompt you to research genetic predispositions to the disease.

Another way to uncover what matters most is to cut to the chase: Imagine that you have less than a year to live. When I was working with hospice patients, I quickly learned that dying patients don't waste time with the unessential. What little energy they have goes into more primary issues than what's on television, who got the promotion they'd hoped to get, or how much money their neighbor made on stocks. They urgently wish to locate lost relatives and friends, tell their life stories, go for walks in the park, or indulge in sensual pleasures they've denied themselves—chocolate, roast beef, manicures, massages. If you knew that you would die soon, what would you write about? What truths would you tell, which secrets would you unlock? What pleasures, denied until this moment, would you allow yourself? What journeys would you take?

A less emotionally demanding way to find your true material is simply to make a list of subjects you know a lot about. The list can include tasks you do well, jobs you've held, hobbies you've mastered, or subjects you've researched. Try not to let other people's notions of what's interesting or important affect your choices. In what area are you an expert? Do you know how to diaper two babies at once? Make your way through a foreign country where you don't know the language? Catch a fish with your bare hands? Have you discovered a way to coax your fourteen-year-old stepson into actually speaking to you? Look at the jobs you've held throughout your lifetime, both volunteer and paying. Chances are you've accumulated wisdom you're not consciously aware of.

You can also uncover hidden passions by asking yourself, "If I could write about only one subject (or person, place, event, obsession) what would it be?" By limiting your choice, you'll be forced to bypass peripheral or insignificant issues. It's often said that each writer has only one story to tell and that she continues to tell this story again and again in various ways. Ask yourself what story claims your first attention rights. Mark Doty, in his poem "My Tattoo," poses the question in another way:

. . . What noun
would you want

spoken on your skin
your whole life through?

How's that for an essential question? Not only must your passion be expressed as one particular word, it must also be a permanent marking, something you could wear for the rest of your life.

Once you've chosen the subject you feel most passionate about, write about it as long and as deeply as you can without worrying about how others might respond. Remember, this is private writing; you don't need to be concerned with making your subject appealing to others. Your aim is to discover a subject so intriguing that you could come at it again and again from any number of angles and never exhaust its mysteries.

WRITING WITH AND FROM
YOUR MANY SELVES

Sometimes in the midst of writing, I discover that—yawn and yawn again—I'm boring myself to death. I'm in a rut, speaking from the same old voice about the same old concerns. When this happens, I remind my writer self that there are other selves living inside me. Isn't it time to let them have their say?

In *Creative Nonfiction*, Philip Gerard suggests that one way to discover new material is to write down five or ten identities that describe you (father, son, Catholic, etc.) and then explore what each of these identities cares about, worries about, or thinks about. My list, which is longer than the one Gerard suggests, looks something like this: aunt, daughter, niece, wife, sister, friend, gardener, hospice volunteer, backup gospel singer, military brat, teacher, hiker, weight lifter, cat lover, cook. Each of these identities has a slightly different take on things and can teach me, the sometimes bored or boring writer, something new.

If you want to expand the scope of private writing, try making a list of all the identities that describe you. Include your past identities. For instance, I am no longer, strictly speaking, a granddaughter, since my grandparents are dead. And I am no longer a military wife, though at one time I was. I was also a proofreader, a second-grade teacher, a door-to-door Avon salesperson, a community theater actress, and a church organist. However, since these identities are still part of my experience, if only in memory, writing from the vantage point of these identities illuminates present-day experience, brings past events forward, and prompts me to explore subjects and passions that lie just beneath the surface.

Once you've listed the various identities that define you, write from the point of view of one or more of these identities. What does the father in you think about the upcoming presidential election? How does the sculptor in you want to vote? Maybe each will pull a different lever in the voting booth; maybe they'll argue with each other. Try writing a conversation between two of your alternate selves. Coax your wild, pot-smoking teenager past to write a letter to your buttoned-down accountant present. Or write a poem to the old woman you will become.

Some of the identities that define us are those we've assumed only in dreams or imagination. It can be argued that our lives are as much a product of what we choose *not* to do as what we actually do. The lives we don't live inform the lives we live, and sometimes even haunt them. So rather than always writing the diary of your lived life, consider writing the diary of your unlived lives. If your name were Betty Ann rather than Isabella, how would you move differently through your days? Who might you have married had you taken that bus to Colorado rather than flying to Phoenix? What *didn't* you do today? Which woman didn't you kiss, which child didn't you put to bed, which job didn't you go to? Robert Bly's poem "Clothespins" begins:

I'd like to have spent my life making
Clothespins. Nothing would be harmed.

Can you imagine spending your life in some different pursuit? If so, write about it. Step out of your skin and see new possibilities.

Writing a diary of unlived lives isn't necessarily an admission that your life isn't fulfilling. It may be a healthy expression of wishes, fantasies, and dreams. However, if feelings of sadness, anger, or resentment arise during a writing session about unlived lives, try not to push them down. William Stafford's poem "Friend Who Never Came" describes a friend the speaker imagined but never found. Though imbued with sadness and regret, Stafford's is one of the most beautiful tributes to friendship I've ever read. Honest emotions, even so-called negative emotions, are at the core of meaningful writing. Our longings, losses, scars, and regrets carve deep hollows within us; writing helps refill the empty spaces.

YOUR PRIVATE WORKSHOP

The freedom to write whatever you want, in whatever form you wish, is one of the many benefits of private writing. But absolute freedom can tyrannize as well as liberate. To invent a world where anything is possible, even the world of your own writing, requires great stores of creative energy. When faced with unlimited possibilities, you may become overwhelmed, unable to write the first word. Or, after writing for a while, you may feel you've exhausted what you have to say; you may simply feel *exhausted*. Like a child at the end of summer who longs for anything—yes, even school—that will give structure to his days, you may begin longing for writing assignments, deadlines, even periodical progress reports to keep you going.

If you prefer to follow someone else's model, you can

choose from an array of systematic writing programs, such as those detailed in Ira Progoff's *At a Journal Workshop* and Julia Cameron's *The Artist's Way: A Spiritual Path to Higher Creativity*. You can also imitate groundbreaking journals, such as Marion Milner's *A Life of One's Own* (published under the pen name Joanna Field) in which she illustrates the usefulness of intuitive drawing and writing.

Though I highly recommend writing classes or peer workshops (more about this in chapter nine), your journal, diary, or notebook can also serve as a classroom or workshop. Within the pages of private writing, you can be student, teacher, and peer. You can assign and complete writing exercises, set deadlines, and even give and receive responses to your work.

Start by making a list of all the writing experiments you'd like to try. A recent list of my self-made assignments includes

- stories about the cars in my life and the places they took me
- a book of interrelated poems about Central Park
- a song for our twenty-fifth anniversary
- an essay called "I'm Nobody, Who Are You?"

Giving yourself assignments can help jump-start your writing on days when your mind is stalled; it can also focus random daytime thoughts and even nighttime dreams. Recording an assignment in your journal is like addressing a postcard to yourself and dropping it into the mailbox of your unconscious. Once the assignment is given, your mind will start looking for ways to complete it. Even when your conscious mind forgets you ever made the assignment, your unconscious mind remembers, the way it remembered to buy chicken broth and celery today even though you left the grocery list at home.

If your mind is blank, if you can think of nothing at all to write, use an assignment someone else has devised.

There are plenty of exercise books available in bookstores and libraries. Simply copy the assignment into your journal, then complete it as you would an assignment given by a teacher.

Leaping off from someone else's thoughts is another way to discover potential assignments. Annie Dillard's notebooks contain quotations from literary sources and the natural sciences, and she refers to these quotations frequently in her writings. My journal is filled with notes taken from newspapers, books, radio and television, bumper stickers, lists of rules and regulations, overheard conversations—whatever strikes my interest. I sometimes find gems in unexpected places. Once, while leading a fourth-grade poetry lesson, I saw written on a child's paper "The truth is sticky, babe." I jotted it in my journal, forgot about it, then rediscovered it a year or two later while I was struggling with a poem about the difficulty of escaping our personal histories. The child's insight about the stickiness of truth helped me locate the central image in my poem, and I ended up using her quotation as the poem's epigraph (giving her credit, of course).

When quotations are used this way, they act as implied writing assignments. You can illustrate a quotation with a personal experience, question the assumption beneath a quotation, argue with it, or write from the point of view of its real or imagined author. I've written several first person monologues in which I imagine the thoughts and experiences of real-life people and fictional characters based on quotations I recorded in my journal: *Peter Pan*'s Wendy, a clay eater, my dead grandmother, an unborn child, and others.

You might also try writing in a journal that has a preprinted quotation on each page; there are specialized journals for hikers, readers, brides, new mothers, students, even stay-at-home dads. A friend gave me *A Gardener's Diary*, filled with stunning illustrations and quotations. Each page's quotation suggests an aspect of gardening that I might not otherwise have thought to include. For instance, the Spanish proverb "More things grow in the garden than the gardener sows" prompted me to remember the wild chicory that sprouted in the tomato garden and the Barbie doll I once found buried in my tulip bed.

Posing questions is another way to create writing assignments. If you look back over your writing, you'll probably find questions you've asked yourself that you've not yet attempted to answer. My journal is filled with such wonderings, from trivial to serious and everything in between: "Why am I so drawn to bald men?" "Why am I terrified of tunnels?" "If the cyst is malignant, will I choose chemo or surgery?" "Why do I paint my toenails red?" Any of these questions, if explored more deeply, might suggest a story, poem, song, or letter I could write. In *Creative Nonfiction*, Philip Gerard suggests that a good question is a good subject. If you're just beginning journal writing, start by asking yourself questions. And if you've kept a journal for a long time, reread your entries, searching for questions that appear and reappear; then write responses to your questions.

Besides providing you with assignments, workshops and classes also operate on schedules, requiring you to get something down on paper in time for the next meeting. So if you wish to create a workshop environment for your writing, give yourself deadlines: By Friday, I'll finish the first draft of the sonnet; by next Tuesday, I'll revise the story about my brother. Giving yourself deadlines not only increases your chances of completing projects, it may also keep you from judging your efforts too harshly. After all, if you have only a week to write the essay, you can't expect it to be a magnum opus, right?

Your journal can also be a place to talk to yourself about works in progress. Gail Peck, a poet and inveterate journal keeper, uses her private pages, in part, for this purpose. She muses on particular poems, wondering if they're carrying the emotional weight she'd hoped they would. She checks herself with questions: "Is this line too sentimental?" "Have I resisted the easy answer?" "Is there a better way to say this while still remaining true to the experience?" Occasionally, she moves from discussing individual poems to discussing her poetry as a whole—noting changes in her work, assessing the progress she's making, and setting forth goals for future writing. Sometimes she pushes herself to work harder; sometimes she comforts herself by recalling past difficulties that ended in success; sometimes she simply talks through a writing problem until she reaches a new understanding. In other words, she serves as her own coach, mentor, and teacher. Her journal is her classroom, her private writing workshop.

At first glance it may seem that giving yourself assignments, setting goals, following a systematic journal approach, or evaluating your own progress only tightens the reins on your thoughts and feelings. On the contrary, using private writing as a workshop or classroom can actually relieve the sometimes heavy responsibility of writing whatever you wish in any way you wish, thereby releasing you to write your heart out.

CHAPTER 4

MEMORY'S HEART

As I write these words, I am trying hard to focus on the task at hand. My mind has other plans. It keeps flashing on peripheral scenes: a lumpy feather bed with iron railings, a sloping linoleum floor, a cobwebbed window opening onto a thicket of bramble and wild strawberry. Last week my mother, after many years of deliberation, finally sold Briarwood, the century-old log cabin where my great-grandparents raised their five children and where their oldest daughter, my great-aunt Bessie, returned decades later to live among stray cats, dusty Mason jars, and stacks of *National Geographics*.

"It was time," my mother said over the phone. I'd known this day was coming. Twenty years past Bessie's death, the cabin had outlived itself, and my mother had no choice but to let it go. "I'm OK with the decision," were my mother's words, but her voice told a different story. I suspect she'd hoped she could hold onto Briarwood until one of us children wrested it from vandals, rats, and weedy decay. I could have been the child to do it; I should have been. Why didn't I? Time, expense, the impracticality of the task? As the niece closest to Bessie, I'd known many Briarwood summers. Bessie and I were a strange pair, seventy years apart but linked through a love of poetry, birds, and long hikes. Each room in Briarwood held a story, and each path—to the outhouse, the bank of Wildcat Creek, the root cellar—was imprinted on my memory.

As my mother spoke, my throat tightened. Briarwood was gone, Bessie was gone, one day my mother would be gone, and there was nothing I could do about any of it. I hung up the phone and cried, and when the tears stopped, I reached for paper and pen. I drew a map of the cabin, the outbuildings, and the paths connecting them. Then I sketched in details from forty years ago: the rusty hand pump that stood beside the low porcelain sink, the tin bucket that hung on a hook, the book of Byron's poems resting on the sofa arm, the slop jar (we never called it a chamber pot) peeking out from under the bed. Memories poured in, as if rushing through a hole in time. The wasp nest beneath the porch eaves was alive again, bacon grease was popping in the iron skillet, a bony hand was turning the spatula.

PLACE AS A WINDOW INTO MEMORY

Once you mentally situate yourself inside a room in the past (or in a school yard, forest, restaurant, barn, or any space you recall) memories will probably flood in on their own. If they don't, try drawing a map of the place, as I did of Briarwood. It can be a bird's-eye view or any other viewpoint that appeals to you. For instance, rather than looking down onto the cabin as if it were an open dollhouse, I might have mentally placed myself at any of a number of lookout points—peering through the broken front window, lying on my back on the feather bed, standing at the hand pump.

As you write, describe the place from your chosen vantage point. "From where I lay," you might begin, or "I glanced up from my book to see. . . ." Try different angles. Move in for close-ups; pull back for the big view. Then, fill in specific details. If you're remembering the high school auditorium where you rehearsed every afternoon, don't forget the worn burgundy curtains, the upright piano, the molded plastic chair where you sat, the music stand that held your marked-up copy of "The Stars and Stripes Forever." Look closely. The smallest window can open onto a memory.

Sometimes the window isn't a visual image but a smell,

sound, taste, or texture. Theodore Roethke's "Root Cellar" opens with a visual description of the cellar, then moves into the "congress of stinks" the speaker of the poem recalls:

> Roots ripe as old bait,
> Pulpy stems, rank, silo-rich,
> Leaf-mold, manure, lime, piled against slippery
>   planks.

At some point in the writing, try closing your eyes and reentering the scene using a sense other than sight. For me, the window into memory is usually a sound. When I write about the cabin, my ears fill: the creak of the hand pump, the clack of Bessie's loose dentures, the skitter of the cat's claws across the linoleum.

When you close your eyes against the physical scene at hand, a window may open into dream or imagination. You might slip out of the skin of the adult who is writing the words, or the child who once haunted the scene, and become the place itself—the junior high school gymnasium, the swimming hole, the den where your uncles played late-night poker. To enter a place more deeply, try speaking from its point of view, as L. Woiwode did in "A Deserted Barn:"

> I stand in Michigan,
> A gray shape at the edge of a cedar swamp.
> Starlings come to my peak,
> Dirty, and perch there;

Imagine the sounds and smells recorded in the barn's walls. What has the barn witnessed? Maybe it once watched a shy, lanky boy (that would be you) picking burrs from the fur of a three-legged dog or pounding an angry fist into the hayloft floor. If you listen to its story, the barn may offer a different take on your past, one you're not able to hear when you're locked into your own voice, your own telling of the tale.

Viewing memory's rooms through the window of dream or imagination is one way of gaining perspective. Another way is to place your present self into the room in the past. Who is this man watching through his mind's eye, the boy in the barn, the boy he used to be? In what place does that man find himself today? Are bits of his past embedded in this place?

Stop for a moment. Put down this book and look around. Make a mental list of every object attached to a memory. If you're in your own home, it should be easy to locate such objects: There's your brother's wedding picture, your grandfather's tackle box, the bowling trophy you won by default twenty years ago, the sand dollar your friend brought back from the beach. Any of these objects could lead you to write about the past.

Even if you're not in your own home, your surroundings can often spark memories. Think back on the places you've been in the past week or places where you habitually find yourself. Make a list of these places. My list includes the Laundromat, grocery store, park, YMCA, post office, library, a friend's kitchen, the subway. Not a very auspicious list, perhaps, but within each of these present rooms, a past room waits to be entered.

In the Laundromat, the whirling eye of the washing machine spins me back to a July morning in 1958. The wringer washer is bumping and grinding, tossing sudsy bubbles onto the dog's fur, and my grandmother is sighing heavily, pressing her hands into the small of her back. Her weariness enters my bones.

On the subway, the homeless man beside me wears the wild eyes and cracked lips of my sixth-grade teacher, Mr. Sheridan, who was finally dismissed from his post and sent "away, where he could get some help," or so the story goes. But not before we students taunted him behind his back and to his face, delighting in our newfound power to inflict pain on the weak and helpless.

Yes, I was cruel, and not only to Mr. Sheridan. My past is filled with cruelties, large and small, and with resentments, rages, and jealousies. When I open the rooms of my past, I can't be sure what I'll find. That's one of the risks of writing and perhaps its greatest power: Anything can happen.

THE COSTS AND REWARDS OF WRITING ABOUT THE PAST

To lose your past is to lose the places, people, smells, tastes, and dreams that comprise the album of your life. Without the weight of the past pressing down upon our lives, the present has no context. That's why the families of Alzheimer's patients mourn their loved one for months, even years, before the physical death occurs. With each lost memory, the loved one dies a bit more. Soon he won't know the woman at the breakfast table or the children gathered around him. One day he loses his name; the next, the memory of his life's work, every surface on which his hands once rested. His identities fall away one by one: husband, father, carpenter, deacon, friend, brother. Each loss is a subtraction of self.

One of the many gifts writing offers is the chance to reenter your life and reclaim, in part, what has been lost to time or circumstance. "To write a life is to live twice," says memoirist Patricia Hampl. The prefix *re*, meaning "again," is found in almost all words associated with memory, suggesting that the act of remembering is also an act of resurrection. To *recollect* is to re-collect scattered bits; to *recall* is to call back, to summon your memories the way a bugler summons dispersed troops. When you *return*, you turn once again in a road you've traveled before. You retrace your steps.

But those steps may lead to sadness as well as to joy. When we write about the past, it's tempting to look through a soft-focus lens, to allow only happy memories onto the page. "The good old days," we say. But what about the nights? To lock the door on the sad, lonely, terror-filled rooms of our pasts is to lock the door on memory itself. When I write about Briarwood, I summon not only the hiss and pop of bacon in the skillet but also the ragged squeal of the cats outside the door, the sour smell of curdled milk, the hollow eyes and mottled skin of a woman whose old-ness both fascinated and disgusted me—an oldness I couldn't imagine growing into.

Forty years later, I *can* imagine it. At times I catch a glimpse of the old woman I am becoming—in the veined, age-spotted hand holding the pen as I try to write my aunt back into my life. I want to ask questions I didn't know enough to ask before, to say I'm sorry for having treated her badly. I suspect Bessie sensed my disgust. Did she also sense my love, selfish and incomplete though it was? When we write about the past, we may discover, as Jung sug-gested, "that the very enemy himself is within me, that I myself am the enemy who must be loved."

There is yet another risk in writing about the past. With each retraced step, you move not only backward in time but forward as well, into a present and future that contains altered versions of your past. Yes, that's right. Writing about the past alters your memories. "Once I write about the past, I will have changed the past, in a sense set it in concrete, and I will never remember it in quite the same way," writes Mary Clearman Blew in her memoir *All but the Waltz*. "The experience itself is lost; like the old Sunday storytellers who told and retold their stories until what they remembered was the tale itself, what I will remember is what I have written."

What Blew is articulating is one of the fascinating para-
doxes of the writing process. In writing, as in life, you must
lose something in order to gain something else. To gain a
written version of any memory, you must be willing to
relinquish your hold on the experience itself, or on the
person, place, or object you recall. This means, for instance,
giving up the notion that you can "capture" your mother
on paper. You will never capture her. Your mother was
made of blood and flesh; your writing is made of words.
Primary experience is one thing; translating primary experience into writing, quite another. Yet all is not lost. Once
you release the notion that you can capture your mother
on paper, you will be free to do what you *can* do: make a
poem, draft a letter, describe the strapless gown she wore
that summer night in 1956, tell a story.

PORTRAITS FROM THE PAST

When I open memory's room, someone is usually there.
Grandpa Clarence leans back on a folding chair, holding a
smoldering Chesterfield to his mouth. My sister stands on
a stepladder, wearing paint-spattered overalls, her dark po-
nytail threaded through a baseball cap. My first husband
paces the floor in wrinkled army khakis, his square jaw
thrust forward. Never mind that my grandfather has been
dead for thirty-five years and that I haven't seen my first
husband for a quarter of a century. In memory's room, they
are as present as my sister, who stood on that stepladder
just last month. The people in my past drop by unexpectedly, in dreams and daydreams; and even when memories
turn sour or hurtful, I'm grateful for the visitation.

The person you write about may be living or dead, present
or absent; she might be a family member, friend, or someone
you met only in passing. Sometimes brief encounters mark
us deeply. I've written several poems about a troubled student

named Achilles whom I met only a few times; I've written another poem about a girl—whose name I never knew—I used to watch in the high school library. The person you write about might even be someone you've never actually seen. Though I never knew my great-grandparents, I feel intimately acquainted with them through family photographs, letters, and stories. I picture my great-grandfather slicing off the tips of his boots to give his cramped toes more room; I wait with Great-Grandma Hattie by the mailbox at the end of the long dirt road.

Picturing the person you're writing about will keep your word portrait focused, helping you show rather than merely tell. If you begin writing about someone without picturing her first, you may find yourself labeling rather than calling forth essential qualities. For example, when I think of Grandma Sylvia, I think of her strength, stubbornness, and preference for action over talk. But if I merely describe her in those abstract terms, I can't see her. However, once I position her in a particular place—in this case, the henhouse—she comes into focus, and I can begin to describe what I see. Set against a backdrop of midday dust and chicken feathers, her qualities of strength, stubbornness, and definitive action will shine forth on their own.

If I go a step further by setting my grandmother in motion, the memory will come into even sharper focus. In writing as in life, actions speak louder than words: Now my grandmother is reaching for the chicken's neck; now I hear the snap of cartilage and bone; now I am following her across the yard to the house, a sunburned child in shorts and sneakers, hurrying to keep up.

As you write about people in your past, try to picture them in particular settings. Think of these settings as backdrops for your word portraits. You might picture your daughter in the swimming pool, your buddy at the racetrack, or your ex-lover in the kitchen. Jotting down a phrase or working title to suggest both the person and the place will keep you fastened to the memory: "Linda sleeping in the hammock," for instance, or "my brother at the pancake house." Once you've positioned the person in time and space, use the lens of memory to bring details into focus. Describe what you see, using specific details: the masking tape securing the bridge of your brother's broken glasses, Linda's bare foot peeking from beneath the long gauze skirt. Or use your sense memory of touch, hearing, or smell to call forth unique qualities. Was your brother's voice rough and hoarse, gravel over gravel? Did Linda smell like cocoa butter and hair spray?

There are many possible poses to assume as you paint word portraits. You might place yourself in the portrait with the other person, as I did when I recalled following my grandmother across the yard. If you position yourself in the portrait, you can describe yourself in the third person, as if you were someone else ("the sunburned child") or you can use the first person *I*. You can also act as the observer, standing at the edge of the canvas and describing the person you see. In this pose, you're on the outside looking in. But you can also write from the inside out, by imagining yourself inside the other person's skin. "I grabbed a neck, feathers flew," I might write if I were viewing the henhouse scene from my grandmother's point of view.

If both of you are present in the portrait, try addressing the other person directly. Phrases like "Do you remember the day we . . . " or "I can see you now" will encourage intimate recollection. This approach is especially helpful when you want to break down barriers of time and distance or reconcile past grievances. I used the direct-address technique when I wrote the poems "Ex-Brother-in-Law" and "First Husband." Mentally placing myself inside the memory and then speaking directly to my brother-in-law and my first husband helped me feel a kinship with them that I'd not felt for a long time. Though writing the poems didn't bring my brother-in-law back into his children's lives or cancel my divorce decree, it did bring the memory of two people I'd lost back into my life, and found is always better than lost. To forget any of the people who people my past— yes, even that one there, the one I'd once wished dead— would be to lose a portion of myself. The spot where our lives intersected, however briefly or badly, marked me for life.

THE TIME LINE OF MEMORY

Mr. Hamaker was the first and only teacher to make history come alive for me. Before I entered eighth grade, history had been little more than a blurry time line, like the one above the blackboard in Miss Sargent's seventh-grade classroom and Mr. Sheridan's sixth-grade classroom and the classroom of every teacher I could recall. Mr. Hamaker had a time line too, a state-issued poster that stretched above the blackboard, but he never referred to it. The morning we were scheduled to start World War II (we'd started it every year since fourth grade but never seemed to finish it), he appeared in army fatigues and combat boots, carrying a rifle over his shoulder. Without saying a word, he marched to the front of the room, made a ninety-degree turn, clicked his boots together, lifted the butt of the rifle, and pressed the rifle's muzzle against the time line, leaving a black smudge smack between the Great Depression and Sputnik. Then he lowered the rifle, stood at parade rest—I knew it was parade rest because my father was a marine—and told us the story of World War II. *His* story, that is, complete with indelible details: the raw blisters on his ankles, the powdery taste of C rations, the soft crying of young men in the bunks around him. "History isn't a time line," he said. "It's the places on the time line where things happened to people like you and me. Good things and bad things. That's what history is."

Though we might imagine that our lives proceed in evenly spaced time lines, in truth our lives are made up of tiny smudges that mark our personal histories. These smudges are not always officially recorded in photographs or scrapbooks or even judged as significant while they're occurring. The memory of your wedding might be a blur, yet you recall with striking clarity the midnight blue mascara smeared beneath a woman's eyes as she passed you on the street one ordinary Monday. When we look back in time, we recall not the sum total of our pasts but rather the random memories we collected along the way.

Sometimes all it takes to call forth the past is to begin with "I remember" and write quickly and freely whatever memories come to mind, in no particular order: "I remember the rats in the subway station." "I remember the yellow apron." "I remember the egg salad sandwiches they served at the wake." The physical act of moving your hand across the page is often enough to get the memories flowing; one idea leads to another, especially if you don't censor yourself or try to make clear transitions.

If you have difficulty calling forth particular memories, choose a period in the time line of your life—say, junior high school—and write all the sensory details you recall: "I remember the smell of new vinyl notebooks." "I remember sitting on cold concrete steps." "I remember the dress with spaghetti straps." "I remember my sunburned shoulders." If even this time period seems too wide, narrow it. Select one aspect of junior high school—gym class, lunch hour, or Friday night football games—and write all the memories confined within that particular frame.

You can narrow the focus even more by breaking a memory into particular moments; I mean *moments* literally. Start by choosing an event from your past—for instance, the day your daughter left for college. Then, rather than trying to write everything about the day, compose a series of one-minute scenes. Think of them as smudges on your time line or as snapshots, sixty-second tape recordings, scenes from the movie trailer of your life, or pages in a scratch-and-sniff book. Record the sensory details: the click and snap of latches closing on the suitcase, the minty scent of your daughter's shampoo lingering in the steamy bath-room, the left turn signal blinking on the car as she made the turn onto the highway. Recalling the event through specific, time-limited scenes will not only help you avoid vague statements like "It was a sad day" and "My little girl is finally growing up," but it will also help you enter the memory more fully.

Narrowing your focus is a helpful rule of thumb for most types of writing, but it's especially helpful when you're evoking the past. When someone asks me to name my strongest memories from the sixties, my mind goes blank. But if someone asks me to name my three favorite Rolling Stones songs, "Honky Tonk Woman," "Lady Jane," and "Satisfaction" come rolling back, and before I know it I'm back in the pumpkin-colored Volkswagen bus wearing a beaded headband and the fringed suede jacket that cost me four weeks' pay. The past was there all along, a bright pulsating room just beyond the door of my memory, but to reach it I had to squeeze myself through the keyhole of specific detail—in this case, the names of particular songs.

The same phenomenon occurs when I squeeze myself through the memory keyhole of old cookbooks and recipe cards. Once I narrow my focus to particulars, whole dec-ades emerge: my cheese fondue craze, the Crock-Pot slow-cooking years, the casserole years when I bought cream of mushroom soup by the case, the cleansing tofu months, the buttery crepe nights, the chop-dice-slice-and-toss-it-in-the-wok days.

If writing down your memories seems too daunting a task, try entering the past through a small keyhole. For example, rather than trying to remember everything about your first marriage, start with the songs you listened to, the apartments where you lived, the jobs you had, the people you dated before you married, or the clothes you wore. Recently, in an attempt to learn more about my father's past, I asked him to make a list of all the cars he'd owned. The result: thirty-seven cars. In most cases, he could recall not only the color, make, model, and year of the car, but also details like the color and material of the upholstery and whether the transmission was manual or automatic. The cars were smudges on his time line; they marked his history. As he named the cars, memories of people, places, and events rose easily to the surface.

In most cases, the more specifically you write about an event, the stronger your memory of the event will become. "If I see it all clearly," novelist Wright Morris says, "one reason might be that I have so often put it into writing, replacing a vague image with a sharp one. . . . Like the observer of flying objects, I was eager to make clear what seemed so elusive on the mind's eye." Translating thoughts and images into words often brings past events into focus, helping you recall facts, details, and sense memories you may have thought you'd lost.

But if writing is a process of clarification, it is also a process of alchemy. Sometimes in the act of writing, you discover that your past has been transmuted. It's moved out of the realm of "just the facts, ma'am" and into the world of imagination and invention.

MEMORY AND IMAGINATION
A few years ago, after reading an essay I'd published about my grandparents' three-legged dog, my mother tactfully mentioned that Mutt had actually been white, not black as

I'd portrayed him. Her comment startled me. My memory of Mutt was so clear that I'd not even thought to ask anyone to confirm my recollection. In my mind, Mutt was black—and still is, despite my mother's comment, which was later corroborated by photographs and the testimony of several other family members. In *fact*, Mutt was white. In *memory*, he still limps across my path, the black stump of his missing leg flapping behind him like a second tail.

Even those of us who pride ourselves on having a keen memory sometimes get the facts wrong. Perhaps our eyes never registered the scene accurately in the first place. Or, even if we did see clearly at one point, over time our mind has culled out what it doesn't need, thereby altering the event by our incomplete, selective, and random memory of it. Apparently I've forgotten the daylight Mutt and remember only the moonlit Mutt, the shadowy form that stood so darkly against the white shed. Patricia Hampl suggests that we need our created versions of the past. Maybe I need the mythological black dog more than the factual white one.

But since my essay was published as nonfiction, I was grateful to be set straight on the facts so that I could decide how to use them in future writings. When I read any kind of nonfiction, including memoir, I trust the writer to be as accurate as possible, and when I write nonfiction, I often go to extreme measures to distinguish between factual and imaginative truths, even while realizing that these distinctions are, to some extent, arbitrary. The debate about where nonfiction ends and fiction begins is a heated and controversial one. Suffice it to say that imagination weaves its truths into nonfiction as well as into fiction and poetry, and every writer must, at some point, make decisions about how to reconcile the worlds of fact and imagination.

Sometimes in a search to discover the essential truth beneath a factual memory, we must allow and even encourage ourselves to disremember the facts, or to dismember them. Of course, a certain amount of dismembering is required to produce any piece of memory writing. You break the experience into pieces, then reassemble the pieces into a new form. This dismembering sometimes occurs on its own despite your attempts at accuracy and begins long before you put pen to paper.

Once the words begin to flow, the remembered experience breaks apart even more. A long-ago scene rubs up against a scene in the present, or a domestic detail marries an alien rhyme, and before you know it the memory has become something less—and simultaneously something more—than you'd once imagined it to be. At this point, you have two choices. You can back up, return to the bare facts of the experience, and try to record the facts as directly as possible; that's one way of telling the truth. Or you can enter the world of myth, fiction, and invention, where imaginative truth may or may not coincide with fact.

If you choose door number two, any number of things can happen. You may find that the words themselves, their rhythms and textures and sounds, reassemble the memory in new and surprising ways. Though you'd planned to tell the story of your lover's childhood, you now find you're writing about the green tie he wore on your last evening together. Actually the tie was blue, but green keeps insisting on being written. Why green? Maybe *green* rests comfortably against *lane*, the word that ends the second stanza of the poem you've just begun. That's right: a poem, for heaven's sake, when you'd thought all along you wanted to write a story. So it goes. One word calls out to another, and the poem is off on its own journey—the poem you'd never planned to write, the poem wearing the green tie which once was blue.

Another way imagination works its way into memory is through a collision of past and present events. Let's say you're sitting in a hotel restaurant alone, years after your last evening with the lover in the blue tie. At your desk at home are dozens of aborted drafts; you've been trying for months to write about the memory, but everything feels forced and maudlin. The emotion you'd felt that night, the complicated mix of sadness and relief, remains unexpressed.

The waiter brings a dish filled with celery sticks and places it before you. Something in the way his freckled hand catches the light takes you back to that last evening. Or maybe it's the music they're playing or the texture of the pumpernickel bread you've just smeared with butter. Your mind feels light, almost transparent, images rushing swiftly from one scene to another. But your body feels heavy. Something is pressing down on the memory, the pressure is building. You hurry through dinner and rush to your room, grab a stack of hotel stationery, and begin to write. To your surprise, the words come easily, and when you reread what you've written, you're excited to see that the sadness and relief of that long-ago evening shine through, though the story is now about a lonely waiter with freckled hands and green eyes. *Pale* green eyes, you note with delight—the color of the celery sticks on the table.

Sometimes when imagination has its way with memory, the original experience you'd planned to write about is replaced with a new experience, real or imagined, as with the example of the hotel waiter. At other times, the original memory finds a new energy by aligning itself with a more recent experience.

One way to encourage past and present experiences to live side by side is to freely mix two or more events within the same piece of writing. Gary Miranda uses this technique in "Horse Chestnut," a startling poem in which a present event—the speaker of the poem viewing a horse chestnut tree through a window—is mixed with several past events. The chronology of the poem doesn't reflect a calendar progression. Rather, it reflects the flow of the poet's mind. The events, though they occurred months or years apart, occur simultaneously within the telling: a boy falls from a tree; a girl named Judy Cole puts five chestnuts into her mouth; a mother scolds the boy for climbing the tree; a young woman named Judy Cole is named Miss Seattle; a doctor administers Novocain; the boy marries; the boy gets sixteen stitches.

In Miranda's poem, there is little connective tissue tying the events together. Instead, the events are pushed up against each other with little or no stated transitions between them. The collision among the events, rather than the events themselves, shapes the poem. What emerges through the collision is a new experience altogether, a reconstructed view of how the mind makes sense of random memories.

If you want to explore the relationship among memories rather than merely record the events themselves, try the technique suggested by Miranda's poem. First, choose two or more memories which seem related in some way—by theme, emotion, character, place, or recurring images. Write about these memories in whatever form feels natural to you. Some writers write one long piece, moving freely from one memory to the other as organic connections reveal themselves. Others write about each memory separately, then later combine the pieces of writing so that the relationships among the memories are revealed. To experiment with different combinations, you might use the "cut" and "paste" commands on your computer. Scissors and tape work better for me. I physically cut what I've written into smaller pieces—paragraphs, lines, or phrases—then reassemble the pieces. The result sometimes feels disjointed at first, but if I work with the pieces the way I might work with pieces of a jigsaw puzzle, they eventually connect in interesting ways.

Another method for mixing past and present is to embed a memory within a more recent event. For example, you might use the moment in the hotel restaurant to transport yourself back in time to your last evening with your lover. "The waiter sets the bread basket before me," you begin. "His hands are slender and freckled. Delicate hands for a man. Like the hands of . . ."

Now you're back in the memory, recalling the look and feel of your lover's hands. Fiction writers call this technique *flashback*. Flashback is a good technique for jump-starting your memory. The present moment—in this case, the hotel dinner—can help you remember details you might have forgotten. When used well, flashback illuminates both the present and the past. The present moment shines a light on the past; the past throws its light onto the present. Unfortunately, sometimes when I attempt flashback, I end up shortchanging both moments, especially the present one, which becomes merely the jumping-off place for the memory I wish to describe. When this happens, I stop myself. Why start with the present moment if I'm not going to enter it fully? On the other hand, if what I'm attempting is a full-hearted rendering of a memory, why not start with the memory itself, rather than coming at it indirectly, as merely an offshoot of a present event?

A variation on the flashback that encourages the illumination of both present and past experiences is what I call "the telling of the tale." In this technique, the central experience is not the memory itself but the revelation of this event through a tale-telling scene. I used this technique in "The Tale," a short prose piece in which my grandfather tells the story of how his four-legged dog became a three-legged dog. The central scene is not the barbed wire fence where Mutt's drama took place but rather the swing hung beneath the branches of a cherry tree, the swing where I sat with my grandfather as he told his version of Mutt's tale.

I emphasize "his version" not only to suggest the mutability of memory but also to suggest that there are many truthful (as opposed to factual) versions of any event. My grandfather was telling *his* truth of the event, not necessarily *the* Truth, if such an uppercase version exists. Aunt Bessie also had her version, as did Uncle Leland, as did my mother. And as I wrote the piece, I added my version, filtered through my grandfather's words as best I could recall them, and through my own words as I wrote them down. When memory becomes myth, as often happens when stories get passed on, your writing task becomes not so much recording the facts accurately as exploring the larger story emerging from the telling. If you wish to explore the imaginative truth hidden beneath actual events, try writing the story of the tale-telling itself, incorporating not only your version of the memory but the teller's version as well.

When you release fact for fact's sake, you may be granted new eyes to see what could never be seen within the context of a factual world. Though your first vivid memory might be of the wooden sled you received on your ninth Christmas, once you switch your allegiance from factual recall to myth and imagination, you can write about a memory you might have had, or should have had, long before the sled appeared beneath the tree.

Any trigger can start the process: a photograph, a dream, a story told by a family member. You might imagine yourself into a moment before your own recorded history—say, the morning your mother discovered she was pregnant. You might write the autobiography of your father or your own imagined autobiography, the one that lives only in your head. You might even rewind your life, stopping at an experience you wish to erase or rerecord. Go ahead.

Rewrite the scene, the way the speaker of David Huddle's poem "Icicle" rewrites the morning when he struck his brother with an icicle ". . . for no good reason/except that the icicle had broken off/so easily and that it felt like a club/ in my hand."

Years later, the speaker of the poem wishes to return to that morning, to play out the scene another way. In a world of fact- and time-based limits, such a wish would go unanswered. But in the world of dream and imagination, a world fashioned not only by our memories but also by the words we write, anything is possible. Three-legged dogs are made whole, ex-spouses join us at the banquet table, and ancient aunts appear at the doorways of abandoned cabins, gesturing for us to come inside.

CHAPTER 5

THE STATE OF THE HEART

Ever since the first picture was carved into a cave wall, human beings have searched for words and symbols to express love, hate, anger, fear, happiness, grief, and every other state of the human heart. We're still searching. Writing is, in part, an attempt to express our most passionate feelings, to give voice to what had before been voiceless. But writing is not merely an expressive act; it's also an instructive one, not only to others who may read our words but also to ourselves. Writing can help us locate the center of our emotions, navigate the passages of our lives, and reflect on the meaning of our experience.

This chapter deals with writing honestly and effectively about the most emotional experiences of our lives, the highs as well as the lows. I begin with the broken heart—ways to write in the midst of loss, illness, grief, and anger—as well as how to look back on difficulties over a distance of time and space. I also discuss techniques for writing about the joyful moments of our lives without resorting to sentimentality or cliché and suggest ways to transform our experiences through the power of the imagination.

WRITING AS A COMPASS

"I wrote my way through the horror of my son's suicide, as if to chart a wilderness," writes Melanie Peter in her preface to *Words Against the Cold*, a series of journal entries she compiled five years after Brian's death. Melanie began writing almost immediately after her son died, and she filled many journals with what she now calls "raw" writing. "It was writing at its most elemental," she told me recently, "because my entire purpose was to use it as a lifeline through horrifying and unknown territory."

Wilderness seems the perfect word to describe the territory in which Melanie found herself. A wilderness is uncharted territory, bewildering in its vastness. When you find yourself in unchartered land—the suicide of a child, the breakup of a marriage, an incurable illness—you feel confused and bewildered. You don't know which way to turn.

Writing can be your compass. It can help you find your bearings and can sometimes point you in the direction you need to go. I emphasize "sometimes" because writing is more than just a way to navigate the wilderness in order to reach some destination—call it wholeness, healing, closure, or light. It's also an instrument that can help you dwell within that wilderness, a place that is both journey and destination, darkness and light.

When you're lost in uncharted territory, you may not know what you're feeling. When I began the passage journal I described in chapter three, I assumed that if I could just write my way through anger and bitterness, I could move on to the next stage of my life. But as I wrote about the events surrounding my marital separation, I discovered I was more afraid than angry, more lonely than bitter. Writing helped me locate the true north of my emotions. If you don't know what you're feeling, writing can help you name your emotions so that you can begin to understand them.

Begin by directly asking yourself what you're feeling. When I asked Melanie to describe how she had managed to write through the pain, she answered, "*Pain* is an awfully generic term—loss, confusion, disorientation. Maybe it's the disorientation that needs to be written through." Starting with a phrase like "The truth is, I feel . . . " may be enough to coax your emotions to come forward. As you write, be honest. Write everything that comes to mind, without censoring yourself. If you feel hostile, say so. If you feel ashamed, admit your shame. If you feel nothing, write about the feeling of feeling nothing—an emotion that is perhaps the most devastating emotion of all.

If you find that addressing your feelings directly is too difficult, try one of these indirect openings:

"I wish I could stop thinking about . . ."
"In the dream last night, I . . ."
"Nobody wants to hear about . . ."
"I can't possibly tell anyone that . . ."

Write until the truth emerges. The words that appear on the page may be surprising, even painful to read. When I uncovered, through writing about my marital separation, that I was not only angry but desperately afraid of being alone, the discovery terrified me. The anger had made me feel powerful, capable of action; it was, to my mind, a grown-up feeling. The aloneness made me feel small and as helpless as a child. I didn't want to face the truth of my feelings. But until I did, I couldn't begin to navigate the wilderness in which I found myself.

EMBODY YOUR FEELINGS

Sometimes it's hard to write about our feelings simply because the words we use to describe these feelings are abstract terms. Flannery O'Connor noted that a writer can't create "emotion with emotion, or thought with thought. He has to provide all these things with a body." The same principle applies when you're writing from and about your emotions. If all you do is label your emotions in abstract terms (fear, loneliness, anger, jealousy), they may continue to elude you. But if you provide your emotions with a body of specific and sensory detail, your feelings will probably rise to the surface on their own.

After my husband's mother died, I felt disoriented; I

couldn't put my finger on how I was feeling. Then my friend, whose father-in-law had recently died, wrote me a sympathy note. "The death of a parent is a trough in a marriage," he said. My friend's description prompted me to write about my own confused feelings. What emerged was a description of our marriage bed as a small boat "rocking toward a port of strange customs," a foreign land where I would have "no coin to spend" and "no language for the crossing." Once I provided my emotions with a physical body—in this case, a rocking boat—I was better able to understand what I was feeling. The metaphor of the boat, like my friend's metaphor of the trough, helped me visualize what had, until that time, been an abstract feeling.

If you wish to supply your emotions with weight, shape, and substance, consider using metaphor. Start by imagining a place that resembles the landscape of your feelings: a wilderness, desert, moonscape, rutted field, stormy ocean, burned-out building, deserted farmhouse, rented room, stairway, stream, or cave.

Once you've imagined the place, describe it in detail. How big is the cave? Is it dark, cool, and quiet? What sounds do you hear? Place yourself within the landscape. Or become the landscape itself, and write from the inside out.

Also consider describing your feelings in terms of the weather or other natural phenomena or as artwork or music or in terms of bodily sensations.

What weather dominates your feelings? Is it raining inside your mind? Is it dry and hot, muggy and close? Is there a storm cloud on the horizon, a tornado swirling toward you, an earthquake splitting the ground beneath your feet?

If you were to paint your feelings, what colors would you use? What shapes? Would you use watercolors or oils? A small canvas or a large one? Would you use a delicate brush, a palette knife, or your own bare hands?

What music is playing inside you? In what key? In what time signature? What instruments do you hear? Maybe you're the instrument playing the music. Maybe, as my sixth-grade student Ernest wrote, you're a "saxophone blazing out a cool melody, blowing out fresh clean air from your soul." Or, as his classmate Julian wrote, you're "the 'Imperial March' played in a high minor key."

If you're not sure what you're feeling, turn your attention to your body. What does your body want to do? Does it want to crawl into a hole, pound its fist through a wall, float on a raft in the middle of the ocean, scream until its throat is raw, pack a suitcase, kiss a neighbor's husband, drive as fast as it can down a country road? Write until you've exhausted all your thoughts, feelings, and images. For instance, if you begin with "What I'd really like to do is crawl into a hole," keep writing until you've said everything that occurs to you, in specific and concrete detail. What will you do once you're inside the hole? Will you cry, hide, sleep? What will you take with you? How long will you stay?

When you embody your abstract feelings through the use of sensory images and metaphors, you are making the implicit explicit. You are providing your feelings with weight and substance so that they can be seen, heard, and understood.

A FIELD OF EMOTIONS

When I say that writing about my marital separation helped me discover I was more afraid than angry, more lonely than bitter, I'm not implying that I felt no anger or bitterness during the months of separation. But the anger and bitterness didn't surprise me. What surprised me were the other feelings that arose as weeks and months passed: shame, excitement, sadness, frustration, giddiness, freedom, guilt, embarrassment, relief. The more I wrote, the more I saw how complicated my feelings were, how wide the field of emotion.

Besides helping us understand our feelings, writing can also reveal the interconnectedness of our emotions, thereby granting us permission to experience all of them, even those that others might deem inappropriate. "The whole range of emotions was mine before and is mine still," says Dede Wilson in a journal entry written two months after her daughter was killed in an automobile accident. In this entry, she writes of a lighthearted event—having lunch with friends—then of walking into a shop where she saw someone she hadn't seen since before Amy's death. The person spoke kindly to Dede, then began to cry. "I tried to temper my light heart to meet her hurt" is the way Dede describes her surprising reaction.

The whole range of emotions was mine before and is mine still. So Dede describes the first month after Amy's death as "shock and disbelief and (yes) euphoria," and as the days pass, the mix of emotions continues—changing, it seems, with each journal entry. One moment she is laughing, enjoying a dinner, buying glass baubles to hang beneath a chandelier; another moment she is screaming her rage to a universe that gave her so much and then took it from her. One moment she is smiling and talking "on and on until I see the faces growing weary and desperate;" the next, she's waking from a nightmare in which Amy shakes her head no after Dede asks if she loves her, then Amy disappears, "leaving two green lights where her eyes had been. They went out. Blip. Blip."

Such a forthright description may stun some readers; I'll admit it left me chilled. But only for a moment. Then, like the image it describes, the chill disappeared, and I was left feeling strangely warmed by Dede's account, as if I'd been taken inside an intimate and mysterious moment. When we're on the outside looking in, we can't know the wilderness of someone else's feelings. But when we're invited in, we are granted new eyes with which to view the scene. Reading Dede's journal, I am reminded that there are many ways to experience loss: "Each person experiences grief as individually as he experiences music, sex, chocolate, cold springs, dragonflies filling the air overhead. Any sensory thing. Any jarring thing."

This is good news to those of us who fear our reactions may not fit traditional, or popular, standards of acceptability. Books, talk shows, New Age pundits, and even well-meaning family members and friends tell us not only what we should feel but also how long our feelings should last; they give timetables for our grief. Newscasters, mere days after the latest airline crash or school shooting, use terms like "healing" and "closure" to describe what can only happen, if it happens at all, in its own good time. I remember worrying in the midst of an excruciating loss that I was experiencing denial when I hadn't yet passed through shock.

And what about acceptance? Maybe some things just aren't acceptable and never should be. Seven years after her son took his own life, Melanie says, "I found a new term for how to live with his suicide: *responding.* I can respond to it, can choose how I respond, but I will not accept it."

When you write honestly, you may be surprised that your feelings do not match the models of grief and loss that you've been given. You may worry, as Dede did in her journal, that you just don't feel things the way other people do. If this happens, rather than checking yourself against outside standards, try writing yourself more deeply into your own particularity, your inimitable oddness. If a strange or startling thought surfaces, don't push it down. Write your honest feelings at that particular moment, and don't be surprised if they change from entry to entry, or even from sentence to sentence. Remember: The whole range of emotions was yours before and is yours still. Don't be afraid to contradict yourself; within the contradictions lie the truth of your experience.

"A LIFELINE OF INK"

Some people navigate the wilderness of their lives through silence, prayer, work, exercise, patient waiting, or simply by placing one foot in front of the other. But those who reach for pen and paper seem to have no choice in the matter: They *must* write. Melanie is a painter as well as a writer, but for some reason she still doesn't understand, in the weeks following her son's suicide she felt no need to paint her way through the pain. But she did feel compelled to write. The words, as she describes it, formed "a lifeline of ink" as she wrote.

Some people wait until the event has played itself out, the emotions have cooled, before putting words on the page. Others, like Melanie, write in the midst of life-changing events, while emotions are roiling and seething. Twenty-four hours after receiving news of the massive heart attack that claimed his father's life, David Dickson was faced with writing his father's obituary. In an essay entitled, appropriately, "Deadlines," David recalls the task, using words like *dazed* and *shattered* to describe his emotions as he wrote. Writing about his father in the past tense, he says, was particularly devastating, since David was still "reeling with disbelief."

Writing in the midst of trauma, within the immediate now of our suffering, can be difficult, even excruciating. But it can also be a source of comfort; the page can serve as a listening ear. Dede Wilson describes the journal she kept following her daughter's death as "a secret companion to whom I could reveal anything I was feeling, and from whom I should not endure a response." Even those closest to us don't always know how to listen to our pain. They may be lost in their own wilderness, or they may be so eager to help that they start giving advice we can't possibly take. What we need to say may be too difficult for them to hear. At one point in Melanie's journal about her son's suicide, she writes, "No failure seems more absolute than the failure to raise a child who wants his life." Had Melanie voiced such a bald, honest thought to her friends or family, they might have rushed to comfort her, to try to assuage her guilt. The page simply listened.

Listening is what a page does best. It accepts, without expectation or judgment. It allows you to have your say. Having your say is more than just an emotional release. It's also a way of reclaiming power. "It was important," Melanie says, "to believe I was capable of telling the pain." In telling her pain, Melanie was talking back to the pain, standing nose to nose with it. When life takes something from you— a loved one, your health, a primary relationship—you may feel powerless, beaten down, incapable of action. To some extent, this is a natural response which should be allowed, perhaps even encouraged. But when you feel the need to act, writing offers a way to reclaim some of the power you lost along the way.

A further notion is embedded in Melanie's description. By telling her pain, by putting it into words, Melanie was remaking the experience. Though she could not bring her son back, she could at least place one word on the page, then another and another. She could participate in a creative act. In her memoir *Teacher*, Sylvia Ashton-Warner, who worked for over thirty years with children of the warlike Maori tribe, concluded that there are two vents from which energy can flow: the destructive or the creative. Energy, she believed, must go somewhere. When the vent for art was activated in her students—through writing, painting, drawing, singing—the destructive vent seemed to atrophy.

When you write in the midst of pain, you are choosing

the creative vent over the destructive. While all else is dissolving around you, your words are forming. And once the words are formed, they won't leave. Anger subsides, funeral flowers lose their scent, the phone stops ringing, tears dry, but the words remain. In *Recovering: A Journal*, May Sarton articulates one of the reasons she decided to write about the loss of a long-term relationship. "I need to commemorate with something better than tears my long companionship with Judy that began thirty-five years ago in Santa Fe and ended on Christmas Day." For May Sarton, as for Melanie, the planting of one word, then the next, was in part a way to commemorate what was lost.

FIND AN OPENING

Ten years after a highway accident left him confined to a wheelchair, Andre Dubus met a woman who had witnessed the scene. She was the only person he'd ever met who had actually seen the accident, and he was both anxious and terrified to hear her account. Though the meeting threw him back into the dark memory, he could not help but explore it through writing. The experience of meeting the woman, he writes in his essay "Witness," "had so possessed me that I may as well plunge into it, write it, not to rid myself of it, because writing does not rid me of anything, but just to go there, to wherever the woman had taken me, to go there and find the music for it, and see if in that place there was any light."

If, as Andre Dubus suggests, writing doesn't rid us of anything, why should we write about painful experiences? Isn't the point of writing to help us get over the pain?

Perhaps. Certainly I'm not suggesting that you wallow in misery or that you take pleasure in pain. But as I mentioned earlier, writing is more than a vehicle to get you through the dark times. It's also a way of dwelling within the darkness. If you sit in the dark long enough, your eyes readjust. Images slowly reveal themselves, like pictures in a photographer's developing tray. So it is with writing. The more you dwell within the words, the more your experience, however dark it may seem, reveals itself. But if you use writing only as a means to an end, as a vehicle to get you through a difficult time, you may miss the illumination to be found within the difficulty itself.

Besides, it's possible that you will be in this place a long, long time. You may not come out on that bright other side that's promised in songs and stories. "I'll never be able to say, 'There. I'm through this,' " Melanie says. "I won't leap out at the other end and be the person I was." Writing can do many things, but it can't give you back what you've lost, including the person you were before the loss occurred. Even if you heal, there may be significant scarring. And no matter how long and deeply you write about your loss and pain, there's no guarantee you'll reach closure.

But who's to say closure is what we need anyway? Closure seals things shut. Maybe what we need in the midst of life's difficulties isn't closure but *opening*—a new path discovered, a trapdoor sprung. Writing can provide that opening. Through words, we not only find a listening ear and release our most passionate emotions, we also discover new ways to think and feel about our experiences, new contexts in which to place the suffering. "Each time I tell the story of Brian's last days and suicide," writes Melanie, "I place the nightmare outside myself and give it a place in broad daylight. I can bear the unbearable because of words. Words are the nets that catch and hold the inexpressible."

THE POWER OF REFLECTION

It's possible to be too close to an experience—in time, space, or emotion—to be able to write effectively about it. "As long as I continue to inhabit it, how can I see it plain and clear?" asks Harriet Doerr in "A Sleeve of Rain." When we wish to reflect on an experience, to place it into a larger context or to gain a different perspective, we may have to achieve distance between ourselves and the experience before we can write about it.

Though David Dickson was able to write in the white heat of pain and confusion immediately following his father's death, it took several months for the full implications of the experience to become clear to him. Now, looking back over an expanse of time and distance, David is able not only to recount the experience but also to reflect on what it meant to him and continues to mean to him. His essay "Deadlines" is more than an account of raw emotion; it's also what Louise DeSalvo, in *Writing as a Way of Healing*, calls a "healing narrative." According to DeSalvo, a healing narrative, among other things, "reveals the insights we've achieved from our painful experience" and "tells a complete, complex, coherent story."

Often, all it takes to gain perspective on an experience is time. If you wait a while before you write, your memory of the experience may soften, change colors, blur a bit around the edges. And if you choose, as Melanie did, to revisit the experience again and again, to write about it after, say, six months and again after a few years have passed, you'll probably find that your perspective changes with each telling.

To gain further perspective, try altering the way you write about the experience. Change the verb tense of the telling from present tense to past, or vice versa. Or switch from the "I" point of view to the more distanced third person point of view. In one scene of his posthumously published *This Wild Darkness: The Story of My Death*, Harold Brodkey speaks of himself and his wife as if they are characters in a story being written by someone else: "The husband in this marital scene was drugged to the teeth with prednisone, a steroid that walls off physical pain and depression by creating a strange pre-craziness of its own. . . . And the wife in the scene was overly gentle, sickroom gentle, terrified and obstinately hopeful—not her usual self."

Brodkey's use of the third person does more than merely suggest the disorientation of the drugged patient; it also, in effect, distances the teller from the tale. Writing about yourself in the third person is a way to remind yourself that the self in the story—the one in the hospital bed, at the graveside, or at the accident scene—is not the only self available to you. Other selves still survive, intact or nearly intact, in a context larger than this immediate now. The phrase "I'm beside myself"—with grief, despair, confusion, pain, or joy—suggests not only a loss of control but also the possibility of being next to yourself, beside the self who is hurting, dazed, or angry. When you're able to step outside the scene and observe yourself as an actor in a drama, you're beginning to achieve the distance a healing narrative requires.

THE DREAM YOU'RE NOT IN

One Saturday morning several years ago I dialed my sister's number, and my three-year-old niece answered. Hanah's voice sounded soft and hoarse, as if she'd just woken up. She didn't say hello; she just started talking. "I had a dream. But I wasn't in it. Only the beach was in it." She yawned, sighed, then went on with her report about the big waves, the white birds, the sand.

Though Hanah said she wasn't in her dream, she was nevertheless the dreamer, the witness, and, later, the teller of the tale. By describing the scene—the waves, birds, and sand—she was in effect describing herself. Writing about your experiences doesn't always mean addressing those experiences directly. Just as Hanah had a dream she wasn't in, so can you tell a tale, compose a song, or write a poem or book that honestly and accurately represents your feelings without once mentioning yourself or your own experiences. You can, as Emily Dickinson suggests, "tell the truth but tell it slant" through the voice of a character, perhaps, or within the facts of an intellectual argument. Susan Sontag wrote *Illness as Metaphor*, an exploration of the metaphors underlying society's view of certain diseases, without once mentioning that she was currently undergoing cancer treatment or that her father had died of tuberculosis when she was young. Her passion for the subject, though unavoidably personal, was funneled into a work that contained no autobiographical references.

I've already spoken about how writing can provide a form for otherwise formless, chaotic experience. But it bears repeating that, especially in the case of passionate feelings, you may express yourself more readily by writing indirectly than by approaching your feelings head-on. As I suggested in chapter three, we often resist the truth and must be tricked into telling it, especially when the truth is a difficult one we don't especially want to face.

But when we're busy creating the dream that we're not in, we don't need to hide our true feelings, since the piece isn't directly about us. And if the form in which we're working is a particularly intricate or demanding one, we'll be so intent on shaping our words that we may forget to protect ourselves from ourselves, forget to claim our right to remain silent. For example, I often find that writing in traditional poetry forms—couplets, sestinas, envelope quatrains—frees me to say what I'm unable to say in free verse. If you're resisting writing about your emotions head-on, take heart from the experiences of thousands of writers who've discovered, within the very forms in which they were attempting to hide, the truth of their own feelings. Don't worry that you're not up to discussing your divorce, the stillborn child, or the cancer that threatens your life. You don't need to. Instead, write the dream you're not in. Tell a character's story, ask your question in a play, write a sonnet about apples. But don't be surprised if, in the midst of shaping a stanza, revising a scene, or describing a character's face, you discover your own face—sad or silly or just plain confused—staring up from the page.

WRITING AS REHEARSAL

I once wrote a short story about a woman who went to extraordinary means to prepare her husband for her imminent death. Since he'd never lost anyone he loved, not even a dog or cat, she urged him to rehearse by attending the funerals of strangers; she even clipped obituary photos of women who resembled her and placed them on the refrigerator door, next to the grocery list, where he would be sure to see them. "Practice makes perfect," she told herself. Though the story bordered on the absurd and was edged with black humor, the question running beneath it was a serious one: Is it possible to rehearse for grief and loss?

As writers, we sometimes "borrow trouble" (to use my grandmother's phrase), imagining conflicts and losses that may not have happened to us and perhaps never will. This technique helps us enter the lives of our characters, but perhaps it also prepares us for our own futures or at least helps us manage our fears about the future. "Sometimes I write poems to practice how I'm going to live," says Andrea Hollander Budy. One of Budy's poems, "My Father's Sweater," presumes that the narrator's father is dead, though Budy's father is not. "But he isn't a young man," she explains to me. "And he does have Alzheimer's." Writing the poem, Budy suggests, was in part a way to rehearse for her father's death. Though she concedes that writing as rehearsal may not always help when the actual event occurs, "sometimes I just have to write the poems anyway. Besides, I may not be able to write them later, so I write them now."

If a difficult experience is imminent or you simply wish to explore the possibility that it might occur, try consciously borrowing from the future by imagining the experience in specific and concrete detail. Imagine slipping your arms into your father's sweater, as Budy did, or lying on a gurney the morning of your heart surgery or signing the final divorce settlement. Then write about the experience as if it were actually happening.

Granted, this will only be practice. The real experience, if and when it happens, will not be exactly as you'd imagined it. Still, the act of imagining may help you, in Budy's words, "practice coping." Writing about his experience of living with and dying from AIDS, Harold Brodkey said, "If you train yourself as a writer to look at these things—this vulnerability, when the balance is gone and the defenses are undone so that you are open to viruses and their shocking haywire excitement—then facing them becomes almost habitual." Writing about your deepest fears and passions is a form of rehearsal. If you imagine yourself into future experiences, you may not be caught completely off guard when and if the worst occurs. Besides, as Budy suggests, when the worst does occur, you may not able to write about it.

Better now than never.

WRITING ABOUT ILLNESS

During the last year of his life, Chinese writer Lu Hsün wrote an essay in which he detailed an earlier illness. In a scene from that essay, he recalls waking in the night and calling out for his wife:

> "Give me some water. And put the light on so that I can have a look round."
>
> "What for?" She sounded rather alarmed, doubtless thinking I was raving.
>
> "Because I want to live. Understand that? This, too,

is life. I want to take a look round."

"Oh . . ." She got up and gave me some tea, hesitated a little and quietly lay down again without putting on the light.

I knew she had not understood.

Lu Hsün's account moves me on many levels—his self-deprecating humor even in the midst of difficulty; his assertion that illness, too, is part of life; and his suggestion that those who are well, even those closest to him, cannot know how it feels to live inside his illness. If you've ever been ill for any length of time or hospitalized after an accident or injury, you've probably experienced some of Lu Hsün's frustrations. Illness puts us, literally, into someone else's hands. We lose our sense of autonomy and power. We are isolated, sealed into our own rooms, our own minds. Sometimes we are also in pain. But it's hard for those outside the illness to understand what we're going through, even those trained for such work. "Quitcherbellyachin' " reads the sign over the nurse's station in my doctor's office.

Yet despite the fact that no one really understands our illness, we may still want someone to turn on the light by our bedside so we can sit up, have a look around, and maybe even show our scars, if anyone wants to look. And even if no one looks or listens to our stories, nevertheless we do what countless others have done when faced with illness or injury. We write about it. Jorge Luis Borges wrote of his blindness; Seneca, his asthma; Joan Didion, her migraines.

Some writers actually write from their sickbeds. In the last months of a debilitating illness, Carson McCullers, determined to write "in sickness or in health," dictated her unfinished autobiography, *Illumination and Night Glare*. Harold Brodkey wrote as he was waging a battle against AIDS, and his accounts in *This Wild Darkness* are notable not only for their stunning, surprising prose but also for their bare-bones honesty. They go beyond the bounds of mere literary courage. It's as if his death sentence freed him to tell the whole truth and nothing but. As a reader, I entered the hospital room, watched his ninety-seven-pound wife, in his words, "bathing me and turning me . . . Or helping me into the bathroom. I had to be propped on her and on the wheeled pole of the IV. I was determined to spare her my excrement. My head lolled. My legs gave way."

Yet, close as I came to the center of Brodkey's pain, I never felt embarrassed by the telling; I never felt the urge to pull the privacy curtain between us. Brodkey seems compelled to tell the truth not in an attempt to shock us or to beg for our sympathy, but simply to bear witness. This, too, he seems to say—his illness, his shame, his alternating feelings of affection and disdain for the world in which he finds himself—is life.

More importantly, it is *his* life. And who better to tell the tale of one's life (and one's impending death) than the living/dying one himself, the one for whom the stakes are highest. The one who has nothing, paradoxically, to lose.

I mentioned that Brodkey's death sentence seemed to free him to write honestly about his illness, and thus, about his life. But you don't have to be facing death to be freed from outer and inner constraints or to tell the truth as you see it. Any disease or injury that shakes your known world can affect the story you tell and the way you tell it. After Nancy Mairs contracted multiple sclerosis, her writing changed, she says. Becoming a "cripple" (as Mairs unblinkingly describes herself) in effect freed her from standard notions of politeness, femininity, and shame. "My crippled body already violates all notions of feminine grace," she writes in *Carnal Acts*. "What more have I got to lose? I've gone beyond shame. I'm shameless, you might say. You know, as in 'shameless hussy'? A woman with her bare brace and her tongue hanging out."

Even if you don't wish to tell the story of your illness or injury, you can nevertheless use the experience of hospitalization, recovery, or ongoing battles with chronic difficulties to fuel your writing. If you choose, as I mentioned before, to "write the dream that you're not in," your firsthand experience with illness can lead you inside the world of an ill or injured character other than yourself. You'll be able not only to sympathize with such a character but also to provide the sensory and specific detail necessary to convince the reader of the story's truth.

In addition, the physical and emotional isolation you know so well, or knew at some point during your illness, can provide the artistic distance some forms of writing require. Your experience as a "patient"—someone who's survived whole hours, days, or even years in which, it seems, nothing much happened—may have taught you the kind of patience writing requires and prepared you to enter the solitary, sometimes lonely space in which writing takes place.

HAPPINESS: THE LAST TABOO?

"I haven't written anything in months," a friend tells me over the phone. Last year while she was going through a particularly difficult divorce, she produced reams of poems, journal entries, and stories. But now that she's "back on track," as she calls it, settled happily into a new apartment and a new job, she feels no urgency to write.

My friend's experience is far from unique. Many people report the same pattern: They write only when they're hurt, afraid, lonely, heartbroken, or otherwise in turmoil. It's what I call the foxhole syndrome: writing as desperate prayer. When the bullets start zinging close to our heads, we drop to our knees, crawl into our writing dens, and start praying with paper and pen. But when the smoke clears, we crawl out, stretch, breathe deeply, drop the words like spent ammunition, and walk back to our comfortable lives. When I asked friends, students, and colleagues to send me examples of writing from strong emotion, within days my e-mail and mailbox were clogged with poems, stories, and journal entries written during times of sadness, grief, anger, or loss. I received only two examples of writing from joy. Why is it that so many of us feel compelled to write during difficult times yet barely think of writing when our lives are sailing happily along?

Maybe, as I suggested in chapter three, when we're happy we're too absorbed in our happiness to think of anything else. Why stop the carousel when the music is so bright, the colors flashing past our eyes?

And if we're accustomed to writing primarily to vent anger or sadness, navigate our way through dark territory, or "fix" problems, when things are going well we may feel, in essence, "if it ain't broke, don't fix it." If nothing's wrong, why do we need to write?

We may even suspect that writing during times of joy might jinx our happiness, tempt the fates. French theologian François Mauriac called happiness the most dangerous of all experiences, "because all the happiness possible increases our thirst and the voice of love makes an emptiness, a solitude reverberate." Seen this way, happiness is a scary proposition. As our capacity for joy increases, so does our capacity to feel all emotions. So won't we be sadder than ever when the happiness ends?

Maybe our failure to write during times of joy stems from an inability to recognize present happiness. Pain makes itself known; when we're hurting, most of us can't help but feel the pain. But happiness can sneak up on us. As a centenarian who was interviewed said, sighing deeply, "Life is so daily." Most days, I move through my life with little thought of the small joys that comprise it. Nothing's really wrong, but nothing's really right either. Or so it seems. Actually, plenty is right; I just haven't taken time to notice.

WRITING FROM JOY

In *A Life of One's Own*, British psychologist Marion Milner detailed eight years of journal writing during which she kept lists of things that made her happy. Most were ordinary events, like "someone playing piano in the distance." Her goal in keeping the lists was partly to train herself to notice small incidents of joy and partly to learn what happiness meant for her.

Making lists of daily joys is a good way to train yourself to write from happiness. Start with what's in front of your eyes—or ears, nose, hand, or mouth. Look around your home, garden, or workplace. What gives you sensory pleasure? At this moment, my middle-aged cat, Leila, is sprawled across the manuscript pages on my desk, sleeping the kind of sleep only cats know. Her white whiskers are twitching, one paw is stretched before her, and her eyes, rimmed as if with black liner, seem sealed shut. Her slack belly rises and falls, rises and falls, an accordion filling, then emptying, playing a music which is half wheeze, half snore. If I were making a list of present joys, Leila would be at the top of the list.

Second on my list would be the cantaloupe I bought yesterday from the grocer on the corner, the cantaloupe I thumbed and sniffed then later opened with a sharp knife, spilling wet seeds and a musky fragrance into my hand.

Start by listing things that are making you happy at this particular moment. Then, as memories and associations occur to you, record lists of past pleasures also. Entries can be fully formed descriptions or simply a few words or phrases: "the earthy smell of new potatoes," "soft brown hairs on Mark's arms," "ripe pears," "the light that spilled from the fringed lampshade when my mother read me to sleep."

Don't be afraid to list things that others might not name as pleasures. After all, you're trying to discover what makes *you* happy, not someone else. Try not to be influenced by what others have written, especially if their writing includes such clichés as "velvety petals," "sparkling waves," "stately mountains," and "amber waves of grain." If the tornado of dust swirling around home plate gives you joy, include it in your list. Write specifically and concretely about the extraordinarily ordinary joys that fill your day.

One way to extend your lists is to create particular categories of things that make you happy. In her famous pillow book, tenth-century courtesan Sei Shonagon kept lists under different headings such as "Hateful Things" and "Elegant Things." Your categories could include "Bright Things," "Green Things," "Crisp Things," "Quiet Moments," "Dancing Moments," "Things That Make Me Laugh," "Sexy Sounds," or any category that strikes your fancy. These can be ongoing lists which you expand from time to time.

Consider keeping your lists in a special journal or notebook, apart from your other writings. Several years ago, in a desperate attempt to begin writing from joy, I bought a palm-sized book covered in soft brown corduroy, which I promptly named *A Small Book of Joys*. Notice that it was a small book. If writing from happiness is new for you, you might want to start small. It's easier to fill one small book, then another and another, than it is to stare at a large notebook that taunts you with its vast blankness.

If you continue making lists, you'll not only be training yourself to notice daily joys more often, you'll also be accumulating specific details you can use later in poems, essays, songs, or stories. Some of my favorite works of literary joy are shaped from lists—Walt Whitman's "Song of Myself,"

Christopher Smart's tribute to his cat, and Gerard Manley Hopkins's "Pied Beauty," to name a few. Hopkins's poem is a hymn to speckled things: "skies of couple-colour as a brinded cow," "rose-moles all in stipple upon trout that swim," "finches' wings." Lists invite expansiveness and praise. Think of African and Native American tribal chants and prayers. Think of the lusty catalog of a lover's body in the Old Testament's The Song of Solomon.

If you wish to branch out from list making, start recording whole experiences of joy, much as you would record any incident in your journal. Describe the smells, sounds, tastes, textures, and sights of picking cherries, riding a wave, or combing your daughter's hair. Get physical with your writing. Make it, as Billy Collins suggests in his poem "Journal," not just a "ledger of the head's transactions" but also a "log of the body's voyage."

Sheridan Hill's joyful account of a marathon contra dance evening, which she recently shared with me, is vivid not only because of its specific, sensory detail, but also because it expresses exuberance that is primarily physical rather than mental. Sheridan told me that she wrote this piece after almost twelve hours of dancing with hardly any breaks. "My mind was just gone," she said. "I was all body and sensation because I had turned my mind off in order to keep up with how fast the other dancers were going." After the dance was over, Sheridan went straight to the tent where she was camping and wrote. Hers was not the kind of writing Coleridge described as "strong emotion recollected in tranquility." Rather, it was strong emotion recorded as close to the event as possible. Her use of the present tense rather than the past intensifies this feeling of passionate immediacy.

Sometimes when we write from joy, we tap into new and original rhythms. "When I'm happy," one of my third-grade students wrote, "I feel like someone is playing the beat to my heart." Our passionately joyful hearts beat with a different rhythm than our constrained hearts. It's as though our inner excitement spills out of the container of language we use in everyday discourse. The love poems of e.e. cummings are memorable not so much for what they say as for how they say it. And Hopkins's spirituality, nearly orgasmic in its joy, can't be constrained by the rules of ordinary syntax. So he breaks forth into a language all his own, peculiar and particular, full of invented words (*couple-colour, adazzle, wind-beat whitebeam*) and surprising rhythms that attempt to catch, like a bird on the wing, the flux and movement of powerful emotion.

THE BOOK OF JOYS AND SORROWS

Remember the brown corduroy journal I told you about, the one I named *A Small Book of Joys*? I have a confession to make. A few months after I started writing in it, I discovered that though the pages were filling quickly they weren't filling with strictly happy images, moments, or experiences. In the middle of a sentence about the delightful feel of my nephew's small feet walking across my back, it was as if a shadow crossed the page; my throat tightened, my eyes teared. I felt the way van Gogh must have felt when he said the olive trees were too beautiful for him to even dare to paint them.

Then, forgetting for a moment the original purpose of the journal, I turned a page and began writing about my friend's recent death. Writing made me remember a joke we used to share, which prompted me to laugh aloud. I caught myself. What's wrong with me, I wondered. Can't I even tell the difference between sorrow and joy? Looking over what I'd written, I decided that, no, I guess I can't. The two are sewn together so tightly that I'll never be able to separate them. In the midst of happiness, I am ambushed by sadness; in the midst of grief, I am surprised by joy.

Such is the state of the human heart. In the last autumn of his life, Brodkey wrote about waking in "a strange form of fright—geometric, limited, final," and described pain and agony that "wrench me out of myself." Yet two pages later, he said, "And yet I am happy—even overexcited, quite foolish. But *happy*. It seems very strange to think one could enjoy one's death. Ellen has begun to laugh at this phenomenon. We know we are absurd, but what can we do? We are happy."

Holding the small brown book in my hand, I thought about Brodkey and his wife and their giddy, absurd happiness. I thought about the glass baubles Dede bought just a few weeks after her daughter's death to hang beneath her chandelier so that they would catch the light. I thought about Melanie's pages, written seven years after her son's death, in which she describes rain not as gray but as "generous."

Then I turned back to the first page of the journal where I'd written *A Small Book of Joys*, and I added, in black ink which stood out loudly against the blue, *and Sorrows*. Every emotion has its flip side; and every image, experience, and event has its inimitable mystery, which writing can interrogate but never fully solve. The mystery of rain, for instance. I'd always thought that rain washes out colors. "No," Melanie's words remind me, "Rain doesn't gray colors. Colors become richer when water magnifies them. Death magnifies life's colors. It washes over the world and amplifies the message hidden in everything: 'Look. Love. Now.' "

CHAPTER 6

THE POWER OF LETTERS

When my husband and I moved from our townhouse in North Carolina to a furnished apartment in midtown Manhattan, we took only what could fit into our red Toyota. Decisions were excruciating, the old lifeboat scenario: what to throw overboard, what to save? We'd need clothes, of course. And the computer and printer. Enough books to pad my writing cell. The ancient quilt from Aunt Bessie's cabin. Our favorite wineglasses, knives, salad bowl, and coffee mugs. A few lamps. A few paintings.

And the box of letters.

"Are you kidding? There's no room," my husband groaned as I emerged from the garage with the box in my arms. The car was packed, the motor running, and he was scrunched in the driver's seat, a nest of coats and sweaters pushing against his shoulders.

I considered my options. The box contained what I call my heart-to-hearts: a thirty-year-old letter from my high school English teacher, admonishing me for my lazy study habits and encouraging me to go to college; the first and only love letter my first husband ever sent; a thank-you letter from the most belligerent student I'd ever taught; the letter my mother sent on my fortieth birthday, describing the day of my birth; the letter from my parents' minister, a man I barely knew, whose wise words helped to save my life when I thought I had no life worth saving. And twenty-five years of love notes from my husband, the patient man who now sat in the driver's seat, waiting. The letters were my life's library, essential texts I read and reread not only for the stories they told and the secrets they revealed but also for the echoes of particular voices speaking from particular places and times.

I opened the passenger door and removed the box of kitchen treasures I'd wedged under the seat. We could always buy another salad bowl, but I wasn't about to leave the box of letters behind.

WHY LETTERS?

It may seem strange to devote an entire chapter to letter writing. After all, people have been writing letters for centuries without outside encouragement or instruction. Isn't correspondence a natural, spontaneous expression of the human need to connect with another person?

For many people, yes. But not everyone is a natural letter writer, and even those who enjoy corresponding may sometimes find it difficult to move beyond mundane chitchat and newsy reports of daily events. To address these issues, I devote part of this chapter to practical suggestions for making your correspondence more memorable, for coaxing it out of the realm of superficial communication and into the world of personal discovery, the opening of one heart to another. I discuss particular types of letters, including love letters and sympathy notes, as well as expressions of encouragement, gratitude, celebration, and confrontation.

But letter writing is more than just a way to communicate with another person. It's also a way to get words flowing, record experiences, talk through problems, try out ideas, exercise your writing voice, and experiment with various literary forms. The fact that letter writing is a natural, spontaneous expression for so many people suggests its value to anyone wishing to write more naturally in any form. In correspondence exchanged between writer V.S. Naipaul and his family, Naipaul's father noted the charm of his son's letters, adding, "If you can bring the same quality of spontaneity to whatever you write, everything you write will have a sparkle."

By looking closely at the letters we write and receive, especially those that survive the test of time, we can learn much about what makes any kind of writing memorable, since many of the same qualities that make for effective letters also contribute to effective poems, stories, essays, and other literary forms. (I'll discuss these particular qualities later.) Whether you're an experienced, enthusiastic correspondent or a hesitant, tongue-tied one, letter writing offers benefits no other form of writing offers.

First, since correspondence serves both private and social functions, it can help bridge the gap between for-your-eyes-only writing and writing that's geared toward an audience. I'm not suggesting that you imagine some outside, unknown audience while you're writing a personal letter (such thoughts could fill even the most confident writer with fear and trepidation) or that you write with the intention of publishing your correspondence at some future time. Rather, I'm suggesting letter writing as a technique for expanding your audience by shifting your writing emphasis from "self" to "other."

Second, letter writing provides a real-life context in which to place your thoughts and feelings. When you write a letter, your audience is clear and specific. Like a radio tuned to a particular station, your thoughts are tuned toward one frequency, providing a built-in focus for your words. Letter writing provides many of the benefits of interpersonal connection while still encouraging your intimate thoughts to find their fullest expression.

Third, letter writing can help you discover or rediscover your natural writing voice, especially if you're a "people person," someone who is unaccustomed to being alone. In her preface to *The Disappearance*, Geneviève Jurgensen explains how she tried for eight years to write about the deaths of her daughters but was unsuccessful. She kept feeling as though she were lying, because, as she says, "writing is solitary, whereas I was not. I have never been alone. All the same, I could feel people listening more attentively when I spoke of my two elder daughters. I ended up writing these letters to one of these listeners." With the possible exception of collaborative writing, which I'll discuss in the next chapter, almost all writing demands a certain degree of social isolation; letter writing provides at least the illusion of company. If, like Jurgensen, you thrive on social interaction, the knowledge that a real person is at the receiving end of your words may liberate your writing voice, especially if that person is a sympathetic and trusted listener. When you know your audience, and when your audience knows you, you may feel freer to be yourself—to kick off your shoes, sit a spell, and talk through whatever is on your mind.

Letter writing offers a final bonus. Because it encourages both spontaneous expression and focused communication, it can serve as a rehearsal for the writing of poems, stories, essays, articles, and other literary pieces. Though some personal letters eventually find their way into print, few, if any, are written with the intent of publication. However, as in the case of Jurgensen's *The Disappearance*, letter writing often provides an entry into other kinds of writing. The seeds of many of Thoreau's essays can be traced to his letters, and Steinbeck's daily "diary-letters" to his wife while he was traveling across the country became his famous *Travels With Charley*. Steinbeck's countless other letters— he's purported to have written as many as seven a day— served as warm-up exercises for his novels and stories.

QUALITIES OF HEART-TO-HEART WRITING
Think back on the letters you've not only read but reread, saved, and returned to again and again. Why did you keep these letters and not others? What qualities raised them to the level of "keepers," while dozens, perhaps hundreds of other pieces of correspondence were tossed into the waste-

basket? When I review my box of treasured letters, I see that the letters, like most memorable pieces of writing, share the following qualities:

1. The need to say it. A heart-to-heart letter emerges from a genuine need on the part of the writer—to communicate, express, and explore. It isn't merely informative, like an office memo; it isn't a blow-by-blow report of recent happenings. Nor is it an obligatory gesture. When you read such a letter, you sense that it was as important for the writer to write it as it was for the receiver to receive it. In *The Book of Love: Writers and Their Love Letters*, Cathy N. Davidson traces connections between letters and other forms of writing. (Although she's talking primarily about love letters, the same principle applies to other forms of personal letters.) "Love letters fulfill a need to confide, to testify, and to articulate what is ordinarily left unspoken," she says. "The same need underlies the craft of writing." Memorable writing, whether a letter, poem, story, or essay, stems partly from the impulse of the writer to have his say.

2. Personal voice. The need to say it is often enough to propel our words forward and to amplify even the most reticent voice. In her earliest correspondence with my grandfather, written before their marriage, my grandmother constantly apologizes for her lack of writing ability. "Bosh!" she writes, pausing in the middle of an attempt to describe her passion. "It all looks so flat and silly when it's written down on paper." Yet her need to connect is so great that she pushes forward, rediscovering her own distinctive voice in the process: "I know you are yelling as you do when I punch you in the ribs. This letter seems just like one of those punches doesn't it? Oh! Please quit! All right. Good night. Sleep tight. Your loving Sylvia."

Voice is a difficult term to define. Sentence style, content, attitude, and tone all work together to form a writer's unique voice, but voice is more than the sum of its parts.

In *Creative Nonfiction,* Philip Gerard describes voice as "what the reader hears in his mind's ear." The voice that comes through is the voice of "somebody distinctive, somebody you could pick out of a crowd, somebody whose voice you'll listen for and recognize the next time you hear it." Voice is the presence, in language, of a particular individual. One writer's voice is witty; another's is warm and down-to-earth; another's alternates between rapt wonder and wry cynicism. In a heart-to-heart letter, just as in all good writing, the unique voice of the writer comes through.

3. A feeling of intimacy. By "intimacy" I don't mean necessarily a romantic or sexual intimacy, though many letters share this quality. "Intimacy" here refers to a feeling of closeness between the sender and receiver, which is usually, but not always, the result of a physical or emotional bond. (In rare cases, the author may not know the person to whom the letter is addressed.) The minister I referred to earlier had met me only twice when he wrote me his lifesaving message. Nevertheless, his letter possessed an intimate quality. The words did not feel canned or generic. I had the feeling he was talking directly to me and only to me. Reading a heart-to-heart letter, or writing one, is like entering a private room, closing the door on the world outside—other people, other concerns—and sitting side by side with someone else.

4. Time, reflection, and discovery. Memorable letter writing, like all good writing, requires time for thought and reflection, on the part of the reader as well as the writer. Although a heartfelt letter may begin with a phrase like "I'm hurrying between appointments" or "Just a quick note to say," it rarely keeps its promise to be brief or merely newsy. Heart-to-heart writing shows evidence of thoughtful reflection. Sometimes this reflection is a natural outgrowth of stored sentiment. If you've been carrying a thought or feeling for a long time and it's been building in your mind, chances are that when you finally release the words onto the page, they will have weight and substance.

But you don't have to wait until your thoughts are fully formed to begin writing. The quality of reflection can also emerge as you write. Even if you don't know what to say—perhaps *especially* if you don't know what to say—the act of writing can help you focus your thoughts and feelings. And if you're patient, if you keep writing rather than merely dashing off the first thing that comes to your mind, your deeper thoughts will have time to rise to the surface, join with other thoughts or memories, and perhaps even change their course as you discover and reevaluate what it is you really need to say.

A WORD ABOUT E-MAIL

Handcrafted. Handmade. These terms call forth images of objects fashioned with patience and care. I've never gotten over the thrill of receiving a handwritten letter. Besides enjoying the sensuous pleasures of stationery and ink and the inimitable imprint of the author's hand, I appreciate knowing that the author took the extra time and care such a letter demands. I imagine him hesitating, pen in hand, carefully considering each phrase before committing it to paper. And even when the words aren't carefully considered, even when the handwriting scrawls across the page, loops back on itself, slants downhill or uphill, even when the ballpoint pen releases clots of ink and the page is filled with crossed-out and misspelled words, I welcome such imperfections. They remind me that a human hand wrote these words.

Writing from the heart sometimes means writing from the body. Especially in the case of one-on-one, intimate correspondence, nothing compares to the human touch. Not typewritten or computer-generated letters, and not e-mail missives, which have no heft or weight, no *body*.

Even if you could reach out and touch an e-mail, it would bear no memory of the sender's hands.

I'm not saying it isn't possible to write a memorable e-mail. But in my experience, the odds are against it. The very qualities that make e-mail so seductive—speed, efficiency, ease of transmission, standardized fonts and typefaces, the ability to make multiple copies and send them to multiple addresses—work against the qualities of intimacy, reflection, and personal voice that characterize memorable letters. I think of e-mail as the fast food of the correspondence cuisine. It's quick, convenient, cheap, and sometimes even tasty, but it doesn't nourish me the way a carefully prepared, home-cooked letter does. This is especially true when it comes to love letters, expressions of sympathy, and letters that confront difficult or highly emotional issues.

I realize I'm in dangerous territory here. Not everyone shares my opinions about e-mail. Many a romance has been nurtured electronically, and though I can't imagine how an e-mail sympathy note could possibly provide comfort, you may feel quite differently about this issue. If my friends or family members read this section, they may pull the plug on future e-mails, which, I admit, I enjoy receiving. I like hearing from my niece in Argentina, my brothers and sisters in California and North Carolina, and my editor in Ohio. The pleasures of e-mail are many: It's quick and easy to send and receive, you don't have to buy stamps and stationery, and it's cheaper than long-distance phone calls. Plus, the fact that e-mail is instant communication means that I can give or receive immediate responses. Yesterday my friend in Florida e-mailed to say that she'd just buried her nineteen-year-old dog. She'd written to me immediately because her need was immediate, and I was able to respond immediately, as she had responded to me a few months ago when I reached out, electronically, for help.

There's no denying the value of e-mail nor the variety

of its uses, but when researchers claim that the advent of e-mail heralds a resurgence in letter writing, I have to pause. Most of the electronic messages I receive can't be classified as letters, and few, if any, will make it into my box of treasures.

LETTERS OF SYMPATHY AND ENCOURAGEMENT

Of all the letters I've saved, those I received during times of grief and crisis mean the most to me. Along with phone calls and visits from friends and family, these letters helped save me from despair. Someone had recognized my suffering and was feeling, as the word *sympathy* implies, *with* me, which meant I was not alone.

Some people fail to write letters of sympathy or encouragement because they feel that nothing they say will matter. "Words are cheap," they say. "Besides, how can I possibly know what someone else is feeling?" Others pass up the chance to share their feelings for fear of saying the wrong thing. This is understandable. Sentiments are important, and perhaps it is possible to write a bad sympathy letter, to blurt out something that sounds brash or foolish or downright wrong. But I've never received such a letter. In my experience, every expression of sympathy matters. Even the most brief and inarticulate. Even the one whose philosophy I cannot embrace. The only sympathy letters that ever caused me pain were the ones I didn't receive.

Which leads me to believe that perhaps the worst thing you can say to someone in pain is nothing. In *The Disappearance*, Geneviève Jurgensen explains how her grief over the death of her daughters was compounded by the fact that many of the people whose support she needed never extended their sympathy.

There is absolutely no doubt that silence is open

to the bleakest of interpretations. You have to come out of the woods into the open and say: I am here, I know, I have seen, I am witnessing, I am here. If you stay in the woods you are saying just as clearly: I am not here, I know nothing. I have seen nothing, I am turning my back on you.

Jurgensen's position points to a need that most people feel when they're in pain: the need for the pain to be acknowledged and, as much as possible, shared. This is true whether the pain results from the death of a loved one, a divorce or separation, the loss of a job or home, chronic health problems, the pressures of caring for a sick or disabled family member, or other difficulties. Any written acknowledgment is better than none, but a personal letter will probably mean more to the receiver than a card whose preprinted message suggests that one size fits all. In cases of loss and crisis, one size does not fit all. Each situation is unique, as is each sufferer.

And each letter writer is unique; each brings to the task of extending sympathy his own values, personality, writing style, and his own experience with suffering and loss. There are no fixed rules for writing a sympathy letter, but if you keep in mind that the main goal of the letter is to feel *with* the sufferer, chances are your letter will be received with gratitude. Try as much as possible to put yourself in the sufferer's situation, and your instinct will probably lead you in the right direction. As you consider what to include in your letter, one or more of the following suggestions may be helpful:

1. Begin by acknowledging the situation and explaining how you learned of it. Express how you felt when you heard the news and how you feel now, as you're writing. If you feel sad, say so. If you feel angry, shocked, or confused, you may want to express those emotions too. The sufferer

is probably also experiencing mixed emotions and may be relieved to hear someone else admit to them too.

2. If the sufferer is grieving the death of someone you knew, relate your personal memories of the deceased. Be specific; mention particulars. Tell about the times you went fishing together or the evenings when you watched him walking his dog. Describe any qualities—physical, emotional, professional, social—that set the deceased apart from others. Tell what you admired or enjoyed about him and what you will miss. People in grief need to know that their loved one was known and respected by others and that he will be remembered.

3. If you didn't know the deceased, you might relate what you've heard about him—that he was a good teacher, say, or a great storyteller or a devoted uncle. If you have little information about the deceased, turn your attention to the bereaved. Describe her unique qualities, especially those that relate to her relationship to the deceased.

4. When a loved one dies, most of us wish we could have done more, been closer. Comfort the bereaved by reminding her of the things she *did* do—the times she phoned her mother, took her niece on trips, helped out when her brother was sick. If you know any details about the relationship that might be of comfort, express them. Primary caretakers, in particular, need to hear that their care made a difference.

5. If you've experienced a similar loss or trauma, consider sharing the experience with the sufferer. Just keep in mind that the sole purpose of such sharing is to sympathize. Even when you're relating your own story, try to keep your attention focused on the sufferer.

6. If a book, quotation, musical piece, or photograph comforted you when you were in pain and you feel it might be of comfort to someone else, refer to it in your letter.

7. Remind the sufferer that she is not alone, that you are

here to help if she needs you. But don't say this unless you mean it. And if you do mean it, be specific with your offers of help. Say "I'll bring a meal over next week" or "I'll be happy to pick the kids up at school," or "Here's my beeper number. Call me whenever you want to talk."

8. If certain philosophical or religious beliefs sustain you through difficult times and you know that the sufferer shares these beliefs, you might wish to refer to them in your letter. Just keep in mind that your role is to share in his pain, not to teach, preach, or lead. A person in crisis needs your support, not your dogma.

9. Look closely at the words you've written. Do you really believe what you're saying, or are you merely echoing sentiments that others have passed on to you? It's easy to write "Time heals all wounds" or "It's not the end of the world" without testing such sentiments against your true feelings or, more important, against the feelings of the sufferer. Maybe to her it *is* the end of the world: her particular world, that is; the world she knew before the death, the divorce, the loss of her health or home. Try as much as possible to imagine the sufferer's state of mind. Simple, honest statements such as "I am sorry for your loss" or "It's hard for me to imagine how sad you must feel" are usually more comforting than maxims.

10. Since most of us feel uncomfortable in the presence of someone else's pain, we sometimes alleviate our discomfort by trying to cheer the sufferer up, to hurry her to a sunnier place. If you notice that you're doing this in your letter, remind yourself that when you try to talk someone out of their feelings, you are discounting those feelings. Sympathy means acknowledging someone's pain and sharing it, not trying to take it away.

However, when someone is suffering devastating depression or is threatening suicide, you may need to intervene with forceful encouragement. Certainly not all such interventions succeed, but often they do. William Styron, whose life-threatening depressions are detailed in *Darkness Visible: A Memoir of Madness*, is adamant about the importance of convincing severely depressed people that they will indeed pull through:

> A tough job, this; calling 'Chin up!' from the safety of the shore to a drowning person is tantamount to insult, but it has been shown over and over again that if the encouragement is dogged enough—and the support equally committed and passionate—the endangered one can nearly always be saved.

A letter is only one way to acknowledge someone's pain, and it probably isn't the most powerful means for helping someone through a crisis. "All griefs with bread are less," wrote George Herbert, suggesting the comfort to be found in physical expressions of sympathy and support. My experience as a hospice volunteer taught me the value of the "Three Hs" of support: hush, hug, and hang around. Preparing meals, running errands, doing household chores, baby-sitting, making phone calls—all are important gifts we can offer to those in crisis. But a letter of sympathy or encouragement, one that opens one heart to another, is a gift that the receiver can return to again and again. Long after the crisis has passed, its comfort remains.

LOVE LETTERS

My first love note was from a red-haired boy named Kevin Bostwick who sat across the aisle from me in Miss Ranney's second-grade class. The message was brief but powerful: *I love you. Do you love me? Check one*. At the bottom of the page, he'd included three boxes, and beside each box, a word: *Yes. No. Maybe*. I cast my vote. Our fate was sealed. For the next four days, we exchanged glances across the aisle, sat next to each other in the cafeteria, and walked home from school together. The next week, I heard he'd sent a similar message to a third-grade girl. I didn't speak to Kevin for the rest of the year, but I saved the note. However inconstant Kevin's devotion, his words remained fixed in time.

Though I'd like to think I've progressed in the romance continuum since then, in some ways I'm still that little girl, eagerly anticipating the next note passed across the aisle. I never met a love letter I didn't like, and I suspect you feel the same. Despite an ancient sage's advice that "the words of an ardent lover should be written in sand and moving water," most of us, at one time or another, crave written evidence of a lover's passion. We want words we can hold in our hands, caress, lock away from prying eyes, and read again and again. Love letters can reach across time and space, comfort us with memories, promise future joys, and, perhaps most important, open a lover's hidden heart to our view.

And writing such a letter can be as riveting as receiving one. If, as I suggested earlier, most heartfelt correspondence is rooted in the writer's need—to communicate, to express feeling, to articulate what is is normally left unspoken—then love letters may be the ultimate expression of such need. In most cases, we simply can't help ourselves: We *must* speak our love. Even when our attempt feels inadequate. Even when we struggle to find words. Still we write, if only to scribble "words can't express," a phrase that probably appears in more love letters than any other.

It's difficult to write a bad love letter, and even if you do, chances are your lover won't notice. He'll be too busy basking in the reflected glory of your words. But if you wish to expand your letter-writing repertoire, you might wish to try some of the following techniques, some of which can be applied to other forms of correspondence as well.

Revisit memories

Think back to your first meeting with your lover, or the first time you were aware of your passion. In your letter, recount everything you can recall, in specific and sensory detail. Where were you sitting? What was the quality of the light, the weather? What was the first thing you noticed about your lover—his graceful walk, his scent, his raspy voice, the way he lifted his glass? What was he wearing? What did you say to him, or what did you want to say that remained unspoken? What did he say to you? What thoughts ran through your mind, what fears and apprehensions, what fantasies?

Then choose another day, a more recent memory. Write everything you can remember—the song that was playing, the dish you ordered, or the meal he prepared. The smallest gestures are often the most memorable.

If you and your lover have been together a long time, place your shared experiences in a larger context by constructing a time line of memories similar to the time line I suggested in chapter four. Mark off particular events, moments, and memories that have shaped the course of your love affair.

As you write, the time line memories may take the form of random details, your stream of consciousness spilling forth images as they occur to you. Consider shaping these details into a story that employs setting, characters, scenes, dialogue, and plot. First person narration will probably feel most natural, but you might also try third person narration in which you and your lover become characters in a story told by someone else. "He stood at the mirror, staring at his sweat-stained shirt and wondering what in the world he'd been thinking, to accept a date with a stranger."

If you desire a more whimsical tone to your story, consider the classic fairy tale beginning: "Once upon a time there was a man who. . . ." Writing about the "once upon a time" before your relationship began will not only give your memories the quality of fantasy and timelessness but will also suggest the life you lived before you met your lover, thus opening a door to secrets you may never have shared before.

Tell your dreams

Most of us find our own dreams fascinating; we might even be tempted to give blow-by-blow accounts to family and friends. This probably isn't a good idea. There's a reason therapists, palm readers, and psychics charge for their services: Listening to someone else's dreams is hard work. Unless, of course, the listener is a lover who happens to appear in your dreams in a starring role. If this is the case, your lover is probably eager to hear all the wild, tender, steamy details you might be too shy to share except within the context of a dream.

Dreams are natural subjects for love letters. Not only are they pictorial, imagistic, and revealing of the inner self, but they also operate by their own rules. Daylight constraints fall away, leaving the two of you in a world shaped solely by imagination. Describe this dreamworld to your lover, as Maud Gonne did in a letter to William Butler Yeats when she described the image of an Egyptian form floating over her. The form was "dressed in mothlike garments & had curious wings edged with gold in which it could fold itself up." In the dream, Gonne puts on this body and joins Yeats:

> . . . somewhere in space I dont [*sic*] know where—I was conscious of starlight & of hearing the sea below us. You had taken the form I think of a great serpent but I am not quite sure. I only saw your face distinctly & as I looked into your eyes (as I did the day in Paris you asked me what I was thinking of) & your lips touched mine.

In a world bound by nine-to-five pressures, where many of us take the form of accountants, secretaries, teachers, and plumbers rather than moths or serpents, why not float a while longer in a dream and share this dream in a letter?

Daydreams are good material for love letters, too. Describe the hopes, wishes, plans, and fantasies that interrupt your day. What is your lover wearing? What music is playing? Is a soft rain falling, a snowstorm blowing in, spring wind ruffling the curtains? Are you in a mountain cabin, a beach cabana, a penthouse apartment, a hammock strung between trees? If you're lucky enough to be married to your lover and your marriage is a long one, the two of you probably share certain hopes, plans, and fantasies. Write them out in specific detail. Describe the home you will build together, the children you'll raise, the trips you'll make, the tender or wild or silly or passionate love you plan to make tonight or tomorrow morning or for the next five years. Enclose a love coupon to be redeemed, and soon.

Better yet, enclose a whole stack of coupons. This is a love letter, after all. So go ahead, spill it all: sexual fantasies, spiritual longings, animal and mineral transformations. The daydream police probably won't arrest you. If they do, you can always blame it on the unconscious.

Count the ways
Lists suggest expansiveness, an inability to contain your passion within narrow boundaries. What is it about your lover that draws you to her? If yours is a sexual union, consider praising her body by listing everything that brings you joy, as the speaker in the biblical The Song of Solomon does when he praises, in turn, his lover's navel, breasts, neck, hair, and thighs. Although The Song of Solomon speaker employs similes and metaphors, a simple straightforward description is often a more direct way to your lover's heart: "I love the soft brown hairs on your arms and

the way your nose wrinkles up when you laugh."

Make a list of particular moments in which you feel close to your lover: "I love the way you shake out your hair when you take off your baseball cap." "I love watching you dance barefoot in the kitchen." "I love your lazy morning voice when I wake you up early." Don't worry that such moments may seem too mundane to share with your lover. What better tribute than to be told that your love transforms everyday events, makes ordinary moments extraordinary?

What sets your lover apart from everyone else on the planet? What unique habits, qualities, and gestures delight you? Make a list. Be specific and particular. I recently wrote a birthday letter to my husband, listing some of the quirky things I love about him, including his boyhood faith in coin collections, Green Stamps, newspaper coupons, savings bonds, and all other agents of redemption. I also thanked him for showing me that Tupperware bowls have lids, drawers can be closed, and the shoe at the bottom of my closet has a mate.

If my list doesn't sound very romantic, let me assure you that my letter was received with gratitude and passion, not to mention good humor. (That's another thing I love about my husband—his ability to laugh at himself.) Too many of us go through life believing that if we were just smarter, better looking, more successful, quieter or more boisterous, slimmer or more muscular, freer or more restrained—in short, not ourselves—that we would inspire love. What a relief to be told you are loved not in spite of your idiosyncrasies but because of them.

Share your days
As I've already mentioned, heart-to-heart letters are more than accounts of daily happenings. Bare facts baldly recorded ("I went to the grocery store, then I cut the lawn, then I put the kids to bed") won't be enough to invite

someone into your world. But when you're separated from your lover, even for brief periods, a letter that describes the sights, sounds, smells, and tastes of your days can be a welcome gift. If you're away from home, your letters can be a way of taking your lover with you on your journey, and if your lover is away, the letters you write can connect him to the world the two of you share back home.

Rainer Maria Rilke's letters to his wife, Clara, written in 1907 while he was in Paris, include everyday details of weather, scenery, people, and events. These letters served as intimate travelogues, a way to include Clara in Rilke's life-altering experience. Through his letters, he showed her the Place de la Concorde, green-black trees along the Champs-Elysées, old hotels with white-gray shutters, cats sitting in bookstore windows, the golden skins of pomegranates he bought at the market. In one letter, Rilke described what he was hearing in his room as he wrote: "Sounds of rain and of bells striking the hour: this makes a pattern, a Sunday pattern. If you didn't know it: this would have to be Sunday. That's how it sounds in my quiet street."

Writing about the present moment is a way to connect with your lover, to bring him into the world you are experiencing. "As I write this," you might begin, then go on to describe the sounds, sights, smells, tastes, and textures of the moment. What do you see from your hotel window? What is the color of the sea, the sky, the eyes of the beggar you just saw in the street? Although it might appear unromantic, even selfish, to focus on your own experiences, if you describe your experiences in careful detail, in effect you will be inviting your lover to share them with you, if only in his imagination.

Another way to connect with your lover is to imagine what he is experiencing where he is and describe this experience using sensory, specific images. Rilke, responding to his wife's description of the October weather back home, wrote:

> Yesterday, while I was admiring the dissolving bright-ness of autumn here, you were walking through that other autumn back home, which is painted on red wood, as this one's painted on silk. . . . If I were to come and visit you, I would surely also see the splen-dor of moor and heath, the hovering bright greens of meadows, the birches, with new and different eyes.

If you're the partner at home rather than the one travel-ing, the daily world you describe to your lover can be as exotic and riveting as a foreign city. Any place and any day, however domestic or seemingly ordinary, contains the seed of the extraordinary: the rush of morning rain off the gut-ters, the musky scent of a melon ripening in the kitchen window, the glistening skin of your infant daughter when you place her on the blue towel.

Break the rules

If you've been waiting for a chance to freely write your heart out, now's your chance. Let out the stops. Break the rules—yes, even the time-honored dictum to rake your writing free of sentimentality (advice which is, for the most part, sound). Love letters thrive on overstatement, hyper-bole, even cliché. A lover wants to be your one and only— the only star in your sky, the one bright flower in your garden. "For I do love you, Livy," wrote Mark Twain to his wife, "as the dew loves the flowers, as the birds love the sunshine; as the wavelets love the breeze; as mothers love their first-born; as memory loves old faces; as the yearning tides love the moon; as angels love the pure in heart." Wavelets? Yearning tides? Such purple prose is uncharac-teristic of Twain, and would certainly be slashed to shreds in most writing critique groups. But in the context of a love letter, such language is not only allowed but welcomed.

So go ahead. Indulge yourself: starry nights, roaring tides, sparkling waves, angels' kisses. A passionate lover may be the most eager, sympathetic audience you'll ever find for your writing. He isn't going to correct your grammar, point out mixed metaphors, or suggest that you do better next time. If he does, you might wish to reconsider your stars: They may be crossed.

LETTERS OF CONFRONTATION, REVELATION, AND GRATITUDE

It may seem, at first glance, that a face-to-face encounter is the best way to share your deepest emotions. But there are times when a letter is a more intimate, human, and expressive way to communicate. In our fast-paced world, conversation often resembles a tennis match rather than a meeting of two minds. Rushed and distracted, we volley half-finished thoughts across the room, then are interrupted before we get a chance to say what we mean. The phone rings, the train arrives, the baby cries, the waiter appears with the check. Not to mention the myriad other elements that complicate face-to-face encounters: body language; power plays; hidden agendas; "he said, she said;" the weight of personal and social histories.

If you wish to speak your heart to someone else, to find a voice for unspoken feelings, or to move through your thoughts at your own pace without being sidetracked, interrupted, or swayed from your course, a letter sometimes serves better than a conversation. And chances are your listener will be more receptive to your words than he might be during a hurried face-to-face encounter; he'll be able to read and reread the letter at his own pace, taking time to reflect on your message.

Counselors and mental health professionals have long

recognized the therapeutic power of letters. In *Letters Home: How Writing Can Change Your Life*, psychotherapist Terry Vance discusses her twenty-year practice of assigning letter writing to her patients, especially those who seem unable to voice their feelings. Some of these letters, like the diary and journal exercises discussed in chapter three, are written only for the writer's eyes and are never intended to be sent.

Others are drafted, revised, and sent to friends, family members, ex-spouses, employers, and anyone to whom the letter writer wishes to communicate crucial thoughts or feelings. Vance calls these letters "confrontational," hastening to add that confrontation, in this case, doesn't mean hostile; rather, it refers to any forthright communication, positive or negative. A letter can break silences, clear the air, and bring into the open what has been hidden or suppressed: memories, secrets, wishes, lies, fears, joys, confusions, and insights. Letter writing is a natural choice for expressing gratitude and appreciation, revealing secrets or personal insights, and confronting difficult or highly charged issues.

Consider what previously unspoken thoughts or feelings you wish to reveal. Though we usually write letters to those separated from us by time or physical distance, don't overlook the possibility of writing to someone you see every day, such as your boss or neighbor, or even someone you live with. Express your pride in your son's accomplishment or your disappointment in his behavior; share your retirement dream with your husband; talk through your confusion about whether to put your mother in a nursing home. Letters exchanged among members of the same household can break old habits of communication and miscommunication, provide new perspectives on ongoing issues, establish or reestablish intimacy, and even change the emotional and social dynamics within the household. The voice that is silent or muted can find its power; the ear that doesn't hear can be coaxed into listening.

Trouble often propels us to write our hearts out. But acknowledging our deepest feelings also means acknowledging joys, insights, and gratitude. Over the years, perhaps you've come to realize how influential a particular teacher was, how your aunt's quiet support kept you afloat all those years, or how your son's wild sense of adventure kept your spirit from atrophying. The next time these thoughts cross your mind, take out a sheet of paper and start writing. Thank the person for what she's done; describe her influence on your life. Don't hold back. Write while your heart is full, and keep writing until you've said all you need to say.

Whether the thrust of your letter is positive or negative, be honest and forthright. Try your best to avoid psychological jargon, labeling, didacticism, or abstraction. Wherever possible, use concrete, specific details. If you're unclear or confused about details, admit these uncertainties, but remain loyal to the truth of your feelings, a truth which no one can dispute.

Explain what you hope your letter will accomplish. Do you wish to voice your gratitude? Tell a secret you've kept for years? Explain a choice you've made? Clear up a misunderstanding? Say so. And if you want or need a response to your letter, ask for one. Tell your brother you'd like his forgiveness for not coming to his wedding. Ask your friend to consider getting psychological help for her child. The response you receive may not be the one you'd hoped for. Your words may be ignored or rejected; they may even stir up trouble. On the other hand, a letter of confrontation might clear the air, creating space for deepened communication. The guilt you've been carrying might be lifted, the wrong righted, the rift repaired.

If your letter contains highly emotional material, you may wish to set the letter aside awhile or share it with someone whose judgment you trust before you send the letter on its way. In some cases, you might even need professional counsel before sending a letter, especially if it contains potentially volatile material such as allegations of past offenses, criminal behavior, or drug or alcohol abuse.

You may finally decide that, for whatever reason, you simply cannot send the letter. If this happens, don't consider your energies wasted. Even if you end up destroying the letter or filing it away, the experience of writing it will stay with you. You will have learned something about yourself, the other person, and the larger situation that surrounds your relationship.

"DEAR GOD. DEAR STAR, DEAR TREES . . ."

We usually think of letters as communication between living, flesh-and-blood people, but the creative possibilities for letter writing are endless. You can write a letter to your dead father, your unborn child, a blade of grass, Abraham Lincoln, Buddha, Philadelphia, or the entire solar system. You can pretend to be someone else, travel in time and space, and even shape imaginary events into letter form. If you alter any of the basic elements of a letter—the form, content, speaker, audience, or details of time and place— you may discover a fresher, more exciting, and more honest version of your heart's truth than you had thought possible.

You may even discover that the sentiments you've expressed in a letter find their ultimate expression in a poem, story, play, song, or some other literary form. "This is my letter to the world/that never wrote to me," begins an Emily Dickinson poem, suggesting that literature is, in part, a correspondence with the universe. The first English novel was in epistolary form, and the tradition continues with novels such as Lee Smith's *Fair and Tender Ladies* and Alice Walker's *The Color Purple*. Leon Stokesbury's "Unsent Letter to My Brother in His Pain" contains many qualities of a letter, though it's shaped like a poem. And Susan Thames's memoir in progress about her relationship to her son, which takes the form of brief, diary-like entries, has the intimate feel of correspondence. Reading the memoir is like overhearing one particular "I" speaking to one particular "you" from a particular place and time:

11/22/99
I love to listen to you eat. Your lips pouch out and I can feel that bite of pear sloshing around in there, it's almost like being inside your mouth. . . .

   I love your hair when you've slept on it wet; the nod of your head that means you know I know what you're thinking; the way your hair smells like a very mild Dijon mustard.

If your letter begins to take the form of a poem, memoir, or other literary work, you may discover that your intended audience changes as well. As a result, you may decide not to share the piece with the person to whom it was originally addressed. Gail Peck's "Letter Never to Be Posted," which deals with a sister's alcoholism, is an example of writing that, though addressed to a particular person, isn't intended to be seen by that person but rather by an imagined audience of poetry readers.

In some cases, the audience for your letter can't be reached even if you wish to reach her. She might be dead, missing, or in some other way inaccessible, like the couple who rescued my sister after an automobile accident nearly thirty years ago. Though she never learned the couple's names, my sister felt compelled to write a letter of gratitude. My sister's letter may remain undelivered, but it won't be unexpressed. As I said earlier, one of the qualities of memorable writing is the writer's need to speak, regardless of whether the message will be received. If you have something urgent to say to someone, say it, even if you know the person will never receive your letter.

The "you" addressed doesn't have to be a person. You can extend your notion of audience to include spiritual concepts, imaginary beings, animals, places, objects, feelings, or ideas. "My Lord God, I have no idea where I am going," begins one of Thomas Merton's prayers in *Thoughts in Solitude*. Anne Frank addresses her diary letters to an imaginary friend named Kitty. And by the end of *The Color Purple*, Celie's audience has expanded to include "Dear God. Dear stars, dear trees, dear sky, dear peoples. Dear Everything. Dear God."

Another way to expand your repertoire of writing techniques is to change your identity as speaker. Write from someone else's point of view, using his voice, style of writing, and real or imagined experiences. In a thank-you letter to her friend Nancy Zafris, Janie McCafferty, adopting the identity of a fictitious Leonarda, invents whole lives for herself and a woman she calls Francine, a fictional stand-in for Zafris. The imaginative quality of the letter seems a natural extension not only of their friendship but also of the camaraderie Zafris and McCafferty share as fiction writers.

As you experiment with alternate forms, you might also consider writing a letter that outlives its present life by reaching into the past or future. Write the letter you wish you would have written to your fiancé the day before your wedding or to your daughter the night she was born. Write to your future self; go a step further and mail the letter. At the end of a writing retreat, Lewis Hyde often writes himself a letter to be opened at the start of the next retreat. "At the beginning of a retreat I often lose heart," Hyde explained to me. "But it always returns. So the 'ending retreat' guy writes a letter to the 'beginning retreat' guy, reminding him of the process, reminding him to be patient."

All letters, to some extent, are time capsules, but some letters project further into the future than others. When she was forty, during an airline flight to St. Louis, Anne Sexton wrote a letter to her daughter Linda in which she recalled her own mother and imagined Linda "someday flying somewhere all alone and me dead perhaps and you wishing to speak to me." Although Linda was fifteen at the time, the letter was aimed not so much at the adolescent Linda as at Linda's future self. "I love you, 40-year-old Linda," writes Sexton, "and I love what you do, what you find, what you are!"

Consider writing a letter that might be read or reread years from today, perhaps even after you are dead. Throw your voice into the future. Even if the recipient reads the letter immediately, as Linda Sexton did the letter from her mother, she might return to it years, even decades later. A letter written toward a future time can provide wisdom, comfort, and insight to its recipient.

Any letter that survives the test of time may take on a life larger than what its author originally intended. Rainer Maria Rilke's letters to an unknown student poet, Franz Zaver Kappus, became a treatise on poetry and love that the literary world now knows as Letters to a Young Poet. Vincent van Gogh's letters to his brother Theo celebrate not just painting but all creative endeavors. And the volumes of correspondence—in the words of soldiers, artists, politicians, slaves, prisoners, famous and ordinary citizens alike—that fill library shelves serve not only as historical and cultural documents but also as testament to the ancient and ongoing need for one heart to open itself to another.

CHAPTER 7

THE WRITER AS *WE*

Most of this book has been concerned with the writer as "I." We've discussed, among other issues, discovering your own voice, writing your way into self-understanding, and writing your way out of grief, confusion, and despair. These are all important concerns that should not be overlooked on your writing journey. But somewhere along the way, you might wish to consider not only the "I" of writing but also the "we." This may require some adjustment in your thinking; it did in mine.

For many years I considered writing as a strictly solitary act. It was something I did by myself, period. Anything else was a kind of cheating. Writing meant locking myself away and going it alone.

And going it alone, I assumed, demanded not only that I write in isolation but also that I draw a firm line between writing and the rest of my life. I saw my writing self as separate from, and even in opposition to, my other selves: wife, teacher, stepmother, sister, gardener, musician, aunt, and friend. Any time spent writing, I figured, was time subtracted from family, friends, job, hobbies, and social and community responsibilities.

Which led me to feel guilty, as so many writers do. What kind of an aunt am I, to work on a poem rather than to go to my niece's soccer game? How can I justify spending six hours revising a story when I could be volunteering at the soup kitchen, handing out blankets to the homeless, or taking care of a sick neighbor? And the guilt was nothing compared to the loneliness and frustration I often felt while going it alone. "If I could just read this poem aloud to someone," I'd think. Or, "If Jim were here to help me with the next paragraph, together we could finish this essay."

These weren't excuses for not writing. Believe me, I know excuses, and these weren't excuses. They were pleas for companionship, collaboration, and partnership; I just didn't know it yet. Before I discovered the "we" of writing, it didn't occur to me that writing could be a communal act—that I could work with a partner in a shared writing space, coauthor a text, or even relinquish my own voice entirely in service of a larger, collective voice. Nor did I see that my writing life enriched my personal life, and that my personal life, in turn, enriched my writing.

Writing needn't always be solitary or lonely, nor must your role as writer necessarily conflict with your role as brother, father, carpenter, or social activist. You don't have to become a hermit, shut out family and friends, and turn your back on civic and community responsibilities. In fact, writing can actually strengthen your connection with family, friends, colleagues, and the larger communities of which you are a part; in turn, your personal, familial, and social connections can feed your writing life. In this chapter, I'll suggest specific ways to turn the "I" of writing into a "we," beginning with various forms of collaboration.

SHARING WRITING SPACE

The most basic way to collaborate is simply to share space with one or more writing partners. This may mean sitting side by side with a friend at a cafe, with your son at the dining room table, or with your students in the classroom or in the park. You might be working on a shared project or individual projects. In this form of collaboration, the content of the writing matters less than the physical presence of another writer during the actual writing process.

Scheduling sessions with a writing partner can motivate you to write regularly. If you have only yourself to consider, you might find dozens of excuses not to write, say, on

Thursday afternoon. But if you've scheduled a Thursday writing session with a friend and you know she'll be waiting for you at the library or the park, you'll be less likely to find something else to do.

Though it may seem that being around other writers might distract you from your work, the opposite is often true, especially if you're working side by side with a highly motivated writer. Focus can be contagious. When you write in isolation, it's easy to find reasons for taking unnecessary breaks, sharpening another pencil, staring out the window, or stopping your writing session too soon. But if the person beside you is hard at work, you will probably be encouraged to follow suit. When Mary Allen and Jo Ann Beard were working on their respective memoirs, *The Rooms of Heaven: A Story of Love, Death, Grief, and the Afterlife* and *The Boys of My Youth*, they often did timed writings together then shared their efforts aloud. Call it what you will—peer pressure, shared energy, communal bond—there's something to be said for being in the presence of others who are engaged in a similar task.

It's a good idea to lay down ground rules before engaging in any shared writing experience, but ground rules are especially important if you're sharing space with a writer less experienced or motivated than you are, someone who has a tendency to talk too much or interrupt, or friends or family members whose close relationship with you may complicate the writing situation. For instance, you and your partners might agree in advance to write for a specified time, to complete a particular task before stopping for a break, or simply to work quietly, side by side, without interrupting each other. Every writing situation requires a different set of guidelines. Decide on yours, and make your expectations clear to those who share your writing space.

GROUP WRITING

In this method, you work with at least one partner, and often many partners, to compose a single text. Writing partners usually share a common bond, interest, or goal. They might be family members, co-workers, members of a club or church, cancer survivors, neighbors, or fellow students. The writing that's produced is a group effort. Its voice is a group voice—the voice of the choir, so to speak—rather than the voice of any solo member.

Because social interaction is an important element of group writing, the method requires that all contributors be physically present during the writing session. (Or electronically present: A computer chat room can serve as your writing room.) Usually the subject or theme is decided in advance, but you can also use group writing as a way to discover a subject or merely to experiment with a particular writing technique. Group writing can take many forms: a poem, story, editorial, dedication, memorial, hymn, prayer, script, letter, even an obituary. Almost any form of writing you do alone can also be done with a group, though longer forms will require a longer writing session or even multiple sessions.

Small-group writing

Small-group collaborations allow for everyone's voice to be heard. Each member of the group contributes to the collective product. This may mean simply talking through ideas or in some cases actually composing aloud together, word by word, line by line. The small-group technique works for many kinds of writing, but is especially successful with writing intended to be performed aloud. One of the most famous small-group collaborations was among the writers of Sid Caesar's "Your Show of Shows" which aired in the early fifties. The group, which included Mel Brooks, Larry Gelbart, Woody Allen, and several others, met each

Monday morning to begin writing the comedy sketch Caesar would perform the following weekend. They worked from ten until six, and the atmosphere in the writing room, as Larry Gelbart recalled in an NPR interview a few years ago, was "supercharged," one in which the writers pitched jokes to each other, vented their "collective spleens," and sometimes even got "literally violent."

Such a writing process won't appeal to everyone, but it worked well for Sid Caesar's writers, who produced successful comedy sketches each week for several years. Every writing group has its own personality and its own way of working. Often in group writing, one person is designated as the recorder or "scribe." He records the contributions of group members on a chalkboard, notebook, overhead projector, tape recorder, or computer. Sometimes a manager is also designated; her job is to keep the group focused on the writing task.

The process of group writing can be as rewarding as the product, sometimes even more so. Small-group writing, in particular, is often fun. But even when it isn't fun, even when the subject material is difficult or the atmosphere is highly charged, small-group writing offers many rewards. When homeless men gather at a shelter to write a group poem, when mothers of murdered children compose the dedication for a memorial service, when migrant workers make a list of reasons why they deserve better treatment, a communal voice is raised. New bonds are formed; old bonds renewed. Two days after David Dickson's father died suddenly and unexpectedly, several family members gathered to help revise the obituary David had written (revision is a form of group writing). "As we revised what I had written about my father's life, my family shared a collective consciousness, an awareness that it was only the beginning of coming to terms with the horrible reality of my father's untimely death—a circling of the wagons if you will," David later wrote. "By recounting his mortality, and adding to and taking away from what had been written on the page, we were not only presenting his biography in an annotated version, we were using the process of writing his obituary to apply balm to the fresh gaping wound in our lives."

Large-group writing

In some cases, group writing requires a leader who does more than merely record the group's ideas or keep the group on track. A leader is especially useful in classrooms or other large-group situations where it's difficult for everyone's voice to be heard. A lead writer, teacher, or other facilitator can manage the group while also ensuring that the writing gets done. As much as possible, the group leader should allow the voice of the group to come forward.

When I was the writer in residence for a large school district, I played the role of lead writer many times in workshops with students. My goal, in most cases, was to help the group write a collaborative poem. I chose poems rather than stories or essays because poems could usually be drafted within one class period. If I was just beginning to work with a class, I'd use the group poem as an icebreaker, a way not only to introduce poetry (some students had never written a poem and had no idea how to begin) but also to foster a feeling of community among the students. If I'd been with the class for several sessions, I would sometimes use the group poem as a way of practicing a certain technique or applying a concept we'd been studying.

Sometimes a student suggested the idea for the poem; sometimes the idea emerged organically from the classroom situation. The students had just come in from a fire drill, say, or were preparing for the state math test or were trying to decide what to do for their science projects. In one fourth-grade class, the students had just completed an art project where they'd drawn family portraits. When one boy showed me his portrait, I commented on all the different hair colors and styles. "Yeah," he said. "I guess we could write a poem about my family's hair, huh?"

That's how the group poem began. After the students shared their portraits with each other, we talked about what we saw in the portraits. One girl said that her mom's hair looked like it was on fire. I wrote the simile on the board and asked if anyone wanted to contribute a poetry line using the idea of fire.

"Her hair is like a bonfire," one student said.

"It's yellow and red," said another.

Another student, who loved rhyme, added "flaming around her head."

Rhyme is tricky to work with, and I hadn't especially wanted to use it in the group poem, but because this was their poem rather than mine, I put both lines on the blackboard and the class worked together until we had a rhyming couplet (another term we'd been studying) that everyone agreed upon.

The ideas for the rest of the poem came from the students' contributions. One girl said her brother's hair looked like a lawn, another girl said her sister's braids looked like licorice. I wrote all the ideas on the board. Then, using the rhyming couplet form that was already set in motion, we began composing lines. We worked for about thirty minutes, and it *was* work. We threw out many lines, revised others, rearranged the order of lines, and read the draft aloud to see how it sounded. The students were pleased with the draft, which we completed just before the lunch bell rang:

Song

My hair is a waterfall splashing over
The rocky landscape of my shoulder.

My sister's braids are licorice ropes
Or black snakes in love, dancing close.

My brother's hair is a prickly lawn.
He rakes it each day with a smooth black comb.

Mommy's hair is a bonfire, yellow and red,
Flaming wild around her head.

Daddy says he lost his hair
Along the way. He's looked everywhere!

But Mommy says, "That's okay,"
And kisses his bald spot. "We love you that way."

PARTNER RESPONSE WRITING

In this collaborative method, as in group writing, you work
with a partner or several partners to create a shared product, but rather than writing *with* each other, you take turns
writing. What emerges isn't the voice of the choir but rather
a linked chain of individual voices, each, in turn, having
his say. What you're aiming for is a feeling that the second
piece of writing, the second link in the chain, is growing
from the first, and the third from the second, and so on.
Each writer, in effect, "answers" the preceding writer.

The correspondence poems of William Stafford and
Marvin Bell demonstrate the partner response method.
Stafford began the exchange by writing a poem and sending it to Bell, who responded by writing a poem loosely
linked to Stafford's; Stafford responded by writing a poem
linked to Bell's, and so the process continued. In his preface to *Segues: A Correspondence in Poetry*, Stafford describes
their collaborative process as "playing annie-over with
poems, . . . lofting one to a partner over the miles, and
then waiting to see what would come back. . . . We wrote
the poems and sent them off, waiting for the rebound and
finding each time that what came back was a furthering of

what had gone before and an invitation for the next move."

The partner response method, which works well for pairs of writers, can also be used with groups, large or small. I often use circle chain writing, a variation of partner response, when I conduct workshops. Everyone in the circle begins by writing the first line of a poem or story; then we each pass our paper to the person next to us, who reads what we've written and adds another line, then passes it on to the next person. Sometimes we set rules for ourselves: Each line must contain a color or an animal or the name of a famous person, for instance. Other times we simply write whatever comes to mind, the only stipulation being that what we write must be linked, in some way, to the preceding writer's line. This exercise is similar to the party game *renga*, which originated in Japan about a thousand years ago. As few as two poets or as many as two hundred would gather to compose long, image-filled poems written in alternating stanzas of two lines and three lines. The poets took turns writing the stanzas, each of which linked to the one before it, but not to the one before that. The chain of linked images that emerged formed the *renga*, a single poem with multiple authors.

Poetry isn't the only form that works well for partner response. You can pair up with one or more partners to compose a novel, play, or story, taking turns writing chapters or scenes. An interesting example of partner response is *Naked Came the Manatee*, a novel in thirteen chapters written serially by thirteen Florida writers, including John Dufresne, Dave Barry, and Edna Buchanan. One writer wrote the first chapter, then passed the chapter onto the next writer, and the process continued until the novel was completed.

Collective memoirs, histories, biographies, and autobiographies are other forms to consider when you're using the partner response method. Let's say that you and several family members wish to write about the family farm, which is about to be sold. If you begin by writing your memories of the farm, your sister could read what you've written and use it as a jumping-off place for her own writing. She might respond by continuing the same thread, expanding one particular element of your writing, comparing or contrasting her memories of the farm, or using any other method she chooses. Then she passes her contribution on to another family member.

The possibilities for partner response are practically limitless. A group of Vietnam veterans can write their linked stories. A class of fifth graders from Munich can collaborate with a class of fifth graders from Atlanta to write a series of bilingual songs. A father and daughter, separated by divorce but connected by e-mail, can write alternate chapters of a book about the effects of divorce on their family.

It's even possible to collaborate with a literary text. You can translate a text into another language; you can write a sonnet that alternates between Shakespeare's words and yours; you can use the first line of a story as your first line; you can even rearrange the words of a published text to form your own version. In this form of collaboration, your partner is a text rather than a person, and your community is the community of literature. (Of course, if you end up publishing the collaboration, you'll need to give credit where credit is due.)

We've talked about writing as an act of discovery. Partner response collaboration encourages such discovery. When what you write is a direct response to someone else's invitation, you can't plan in advance what you're going to say; you must discover it. Your partner's words focus and shape your words. As a result, you may be surprised by what you write. You may find that, in writing as in life, two heads really are better than one. At any rate, you won't have to invent your writing task, since it will be implied within your partner's words. As Marvin Bell suggests in his preface to *Annie-Over*, partner response writing offers many gifts, including "the simple truth of process, the formal implication of deadlines, the benefits of friendship, the gift of attention, and the chance to be changed by another." Response writing is a form of deep listening. Because what you write depends on what someone else has written, you must be attentive not only to what is being said but to how it is being said. And you must be willing to be changed by the encounter.

ANTHOLOGIES AND COLLECTIONS

Collaboration doesn't require you to write with others or even to write responsively. You can also participate in a communal project by contributing to an anthology, compilation, or other collection of writing, or by editing such a collection. Collections vary in length, scope, design, and purpose, depending on the groups they represent. They may contain work from two authors or two hundred authors. They may take the form of newsletters, magazines, pamphlets, or book-length anthologies. Writers can contribute anything from a single phrase to an entire essay, story, poem, or chapter. The collaborators might know each other intimately—as in the case of family or close friends—or they might be strangers. They might write their contributions in the presence of other writers during a workshop, retreat, or other gathering, or they might write them alone at their desks or computers.

Anthologies celebrate the individual voices of contributors while still fostering a sense of community. Each person writes his own piece in his own way, but when the pieces are gathered, they form something greater than the sum of the separate parts. In her introduction to *Real Conditions*, a magazine that grew out of workshops inspired by Chicago's Community Writing Project, workshop leader Cecile Goding describes the process of collaboration this way: "As people in a community write together, mapping the twists and turns of their own complex lives, they begin to see places where individual stories intersect. . . . Soon, a larger story begins to collect, a story both wider and wiser than what existed before."

Consider the many ways you can collaborate with other writers to form a story larger, wider, and wiser than the story you could tell alone. A good place to begin is an intersection point where individual lives meet; use that point as the starting place for a collaboration. Consider these possibilities:

• The intersection point might be a community that's already in place. Start with one to which you already belong: your family, neighborhood, synagogue, mosque, athletic team, music group, gourmet club, classroom, cancer survivor group, Internet chat group. Ask the community for collaboration ideas, or suggest some yourself. Members of your gourmet club could write reviews of the best meals they ever ate; baseball buddies could share their most embarrassing moments on the field; singers in your choral group could trace their musical histories; students in your junior high class could describe their rooms. You might also consider venturing outside your community to build a writing collaborative. Start a writing workshop or create a newsletter at a literacy center, homeless shelter, prison, retirement home, halfway house, or hospice center.

• The intersection point might be a shared event. Survivors of a flood or tornado can write their individual stories, collate their losses, describe their plans for rebuilding. Guests at a wedding, Bar Mitzvah, graduation, or anniversary celebration can prepare tributes, words of advice, letters, and poems to present to the honorees. In the "What They Were Thinking" series in *The New York Times Magazine*, photographs of groups of people (who are often gathered for a communal event) are combined with individual comments by these same people describing their thoughts and feelings at the moment the photograph was being taken. You could apply this technique, or a similar one, to a collaborative writing project.

• The intersection point might be a place. Alumni can recall their years at their alma mater. Families can compile memories of homes in which they've lived. Fellow travelers can record their observations about towns they visit along their journey. Liz Sevcenko, a historian in New York City, created a program called Mapping Memories, which records personal histories as a way of producing a collective history of New Yorkers. As part of the ongoing project, large maps of the city are set up at street fairs, community centers, museums, and other public places, and New Yorkers are invited to write personal comments, observations, and memories directly on the map. According to Sevcenko, some people trace their love histories; some, their history of gang affiliations. Others record their work histories, "so it becomes a labor history of the city as well."

• The intersection point might be a common interest, subject, or question. Consider contributing to a collection of writings by, say, baseball enthusiasts, wine connoisseurs, or amateur geologists. If no such collection exists, create it yourself, as Janice Eidus and John Kastan did when they edited *It's Only Rock and Roll: An Anthology of Rock and Roll Short Stories*. Start with an idea you wish to explore or a subject you feel passionately about, then encourage others to share in your exploration. Ask a question and invite others to respond. *Notes on the Kitchen Table*, an anthology edited by Bob Greene and D.G. Fulford, began as a question posed to hundreds of families: "If you had to write a note— one note—and leave it propped against the sugar bowl on your kitchen table for future generations to read, what would you say in that note?"

• The intersection point might be shared experience. When I review the anthologies to which I've contributed, I'm reminded of bonds I share with other contributors— with women who never bore children, with writers grieving the death of loved ones, with "boomer girls" who came of age when I did, and with poets who live in my city. Any group that shares a common experience—World War II fighter pilots, migrant workers, secretaries, recovering alcoholics, parents of children with Down's syndrome—can compile their individual stories to tell a larger story. And those who share an intense, long-term bond can create, through their individual contributions, what amounts to a joint memoir or autobiography—the autobiography of a family, for instance, or a church, neighborhood, school, even a love affair. Dennis and Vicki Covington's *Cleaving: The Story of a Marriage*, a collaboration between husband and wife, is told in alternating voices. One chapter is authored by Dennis, the next by Vicki, the next by Dennis, and so on. Together, they trace not only their individual stories but their combined story as well.

DICTATION AND INTERVIEWS
When a journalist sends a list of interview questions to a prisoner, when a hospice volunteer takes dictation from a patient, when a daughter asks a mother to describe her earliest memories, they are engaged in forms of collaboration. They are helping others have their say.

Dictation
Dictation is an excellent technique to use with someone who is unable or unwilling to write independently or whose writing skills are limited. Kenneth Koch details his use of the dictation method in *I Never Told Anybody: Teaching Poetry Writing in a Nursing Home*, suggesting the many rewards of this method. I often use dictation when I work

with young children in the classroom. Sitting beside a child, I ask her to compose her poem or story aloud. As she speaks, I write down her words, stopping occasionally to read back what I've written. If a child hesitates or becomes tongue-tied, I adjust my rhythm to hers. Occasionally I use a tape recorder, but I find that the machine sometimes comes between the child and me, breaking the intimate connection.

Dictation offers the speaker a chance to have her say. But the rewards are often even greater for the person taking the dictation than for the speaker, and if you decide to use dictation to record someone else's words, be prepared to be changed by the experience.

Interviews

Although interviews aren't usually considered collaborative efforts, in effect all interviews are collaborations. (*Interview* suggests *inter-view*, a view that passes between two people, a shared vision.) When NPR's Terry Gross interviews a guest, she is collaborating with him. Through a combination of questioning, listening, responding, clarifying, and interpreting, she helps him tell his story. It might even be said that they are telling a collective story.

There are many ways to conduct interviews. You can use specific questions to elicit responses, or you can conduct a nondirected interview, which Philip Gerard describes in *Creative Nonfiction* as "allowing subjects to speak at length about their experiences, free-associating, in effect telling a story rather than answering specific questions." Your interview can be formal or casual, planned or spontaneous. You can take notes during the interview, record the interview on tape, or rely solely on your memory. You can interview by phone, mail, e-mail, or during a face-to-face meeting.

Though phone and mail interviews are usually more convenient and easier to arrange than face-to-face meetings, face-to-face meetings provide an opportunity to record more than just the words someone speaks. In a face-to-face meeting, you can note physical characteristics, gestures, pauses, and silences, which often speak louder than words. Let's say that you've just asked your aunt about her first husband, who died before you were born. If she responds by looking out the window, absentmindedly letting her cigarette burn down to ash, or making an abrupt departure from the room, she is answering your question, though not directly and not with words.

Once you've completed your interview, decide how you wish to use the information. You can either transcribe the entire tape exactly as it is or you can select just the sections you wish to use. For instance, if you've tape-recorded your son's account of his first day of junior high, you might select only his words, in which case the transcription will read like a personal story. But you might also transcribe the exchange between you and your son; in this case, your transcription will read like a dialogue.

You might also choose to paraphrase or summarize the interview, or combine paraphrase and summary with direct quotations, so that your account reads like a short story or essay. You might even include the thoughts and feelings that occurred to you during the interview, as well as other personal reflections.

You might even decide to remove your own voice from the writing entirely, as Amy Hill Hearth did when she collaborated with Sadie and Bessie Delany on *Having Our Say: The Delany Sisters' First 100 Years*. Hearth conducted lengthy interviews with the sisters, encouraging them to tell their stories in their own words. Then she shaped their stories to form a narrative whole. "The sequence of the stories is mine," she writes in the introduction, "but the words are all theirs."

OTHER WAYS TO COLLABORATE

In addition to the methods I've discussed previously, there are many other ways to nourish the "we" of writing, including

• Talking through your ideas with another writer while you're both working on separate projects. Jo Ann Beard and Mary Allen, whose collaboration I mentioned at the beginning of this chapter, no longer live close enough to do timed writings together, but they still read new work to each other over the telephone once or twice a week.

• Coauthoring a piece of writing. This may mean writing together, as in the partner-response or group writing methods mentioned earlier, or it may mean dividing up the workload so that each partner uses his natural strengths to support the collaboration. For example, your husband might do preliminary research for an article you wish to write; then, after you've drafted the article, your daughter could reorganize the information or edit your prose. The final text of a coauthored piece can feature the individual voices of its writers, as in Vicki and Dennis Covington's *Cleaving*, or it can read as if it were written by a single author.

• Collaborating with an artist, graphic designer, photographer, musician, or actor to produce an art book, illustrated children's book, or performance piece. John Lane and Douglas Whittle, who both lost their fathers to suicide, created *The Dead Father Poems*, a book containing poems by Lane and reproductions of etchings by Whittle. Lane also collaborated with musician Mark O'Connor by providing improvisational poems as liner notes for O'Connor's classical release *Midnight on the Water*.

• Creating venues for collaborative work. Start a family e-mail newsletter and encourage everyone to contribute an article, poem, or story. Place a memory book in your vacation cottage so that guests can write reflections of their time spent there. Set up a writing table, typewriter, or computer in a hospital waiting room or chapel, and invite visitors to share their fears and concerns on paper.

• Compiling works that are already created. As a compiler, your main function is to gather various written pieces or oral material that could be translated into written form. I'm currently compiling examples of words and phrases coined by my fifteen nephews and nieces when they were small. I envision the finished product as a collective family lexicon. I'll include, among other phrases, Andrew's "day-mares" (scary thoughts we have while we're awake); Hanah's idea for "please cards," her variation on thank-you cards; and the "knee puffs" that Michael wears for soccer and can never seem to keep from sliding down his legs.

• Editing or coediting an anthology, collection, or other collaborative work. Editing requires more than simply gathering work from other writers. Before you begin, it's usually best to specify certain guidelines such as theme, form, or length of contributions, though sometimes an open-ended invitation encourages a more varied and interesting collection. Once you've selected which contributions you'll use, you may need to work with contributors to help them revise or edit their work. You may also decide to write an introduction, an afterword, or transitional material to link individual contributions and give the collection the feeling of a focused whole.

• Collaborating to complete a project someone else began. Unfortunately, many writing projects that could and should be carried to completion aren't. Writers lose hope and energy. They run out of time or money. They get sick. They may even die before the project is completed. If you believe that someone's unfinished work should be brought to fruition, consider helping that writer finish the work. Encourage your daughter to write the last sonnet in the sequence. Translate your Armenian grandmother's memoir into English. And if your grandfather left reams of research materials for a book he was working on, use that research to complete the project he began. You might even collaborate with your earlier self, that young woman who, twenty years ago, drafted a short story collection and then abandoned it. Pick up the pieces. Collaborate with yourself. Finish the work you began long ago.

INVITING OTHERS IN: A FINAL WORD

Writing is a mystery even to those who practice it, but to those who stand outside the writing door, writing can be not only mysterious but intimidating as well, a process from which they feel excluded. Collaboration isn't the only way to include others in your writing. Even if you choose to go it alone, you can still find ways to invite friends, family, and others in your community to share in your writing passion.

Sometimes all it takes is to invite them into your writing space. The child who gets upset when you close the door to your study might sit quietly beside you on the sofa coloring in his coloring book or playing with his Matchbox cars while you sketch out ideas for a story. And the spouse who doesn't understand why in the world you want to take another poetry class may change her tune once she's watched you revise a sonnet at the kitchen table. Witnessing a writer in action (scribbling in a journal, drafting a story, researching, interviewing, revising, editing, printing out the final copy) helps to demystify the writing process while also teaching respect for the craft.

Of course, once your friends and family actually watch you write or study page after page of your messy drafts, you risk getting bumped off the artistic pedestal they may have placed you on. "Oh, I get it now," one of my nephews said after watching me edit an essay. "You just put words down on paper and then you scratch them out. I can do that."

Exactly. He *can* do that. Though his final product may look different from mine, he can participate in the process in much the same way I do. Once your friends and family members see what you're doing from the inside out, they'll probably feel less excluded not only from your writing but from writing in general. They may even catch the writing bug themselves, and you'll have not one but two—or three or four—writers in the house. Then you'll have a new set of challenges. But that's another book.

CHAPTER 8

WRITING AND WORK

We live and breathe our life's work. We know it inside out. Within our vocations and avocations—as parents, teachers, carpenters, waiters, accountants, salespeople, horse trainers, hairstylists, heart surgeons, amateur pianists, volunteer docents—lie possibilities for heartfelt writing. When you write from and about your life's work, you draw from a deep well of knowledge, experience, and authority. Although most people consider their life's work to be synonymous with their careers, in reality your life's work is more than your profession or occupation. It includes jobs you've held, projects you've accomplished, subjects and hobbies you've explored, crises you've lived through, and the personal and public relationships that have formed you.

Maybe you don't get a paycheck. Maybe you're between jobs, retired, or for whatever reason not part of what society labels the "gainfully employed." Or maybe what you do to make a living isn't what you do to make a life. That is, your life's work lies outside your nine-to-five job—in your evening chess tournaments, on summer kayaking trips, or on the suicide hot line where you volunteer each weekend. Whether your life's work is a career, a hobby, a sport, your family, or an intellectual or spiritual discipline, your experience with that life's work is valuable material for writing. In this chapter, I'll suggest ways to identify your areas of expertise, tap into your knowledge base, explore questions related to your life's work, and use the details of your life's work to fuel your writing.

IDENTIFY YOUR EXPERTISE

Everyone is an expert in something. If you don't believe this, you may have bought into the notion that an expert is someone who excels, preferably in something that our society values. But an *expert* is simply someone with *experience*. If you've spent fifteen years waiting tables, you're an expert on waiting tables. If you've raised seven children or two grandchildren or someone else's child, you're a child-care expert. If you've managed cancer pain for several months, you're an expert on cancer pain. Your experience has taught you much, and you, in turn, can pass on what you've learned.

You might be thinking, "Why would anyone be interested in my life's work? I'm not a high-powered lawyer or the C.E.O. of a major corporation. I'm just a veterinarian's assistant" (or preschool teacher, short-order cook, or cashier). Don't be so quick to dismiss your experiences. Almost any field of work, if written about with passionate authority, can provide opportunities for heartfelt stories, essays, articles, or poems. Some of the most fascinating writing I've come across lately concerns jobs most people would consider, at first glance, to be mundane, even menial: housecleaning, phone solicitation, dog grooming, window washing.

In chapter three, I suggested making a series of lists as a way of discovering material to write about. These lists, which include jobs you've held, subjects and hobbies you've explored, and identities that describe you, can also help you locate areas of expertise. If you haven't yet made these lists, make them now.

In your list of *jobs*, don't overlook volunteer positions, childhood or temporary jobs, and even those jobs you weren't any good at. (Expertise is acquired in many schools, including the school of hard knocks). Beginning with your earliest jobs, your list might look something like this: dog sitter, newspaper carrier, bicycle mechanic, lifeguard, substitute teacher, Big Brother mentor, editor of neighborhood newsletter, high school history teacher, freelance consultant.

In your list of *subjects* or *hobbies*, be as specific as possible. Don't write just "cooking"; make a list of signature dishes, favorite menus, or intricate culinary tasks you've accomplished. Detail special areas of interest and experience.

As you make a list of *identities* that describe you, include not only publicly acknowledged identities (sister, wife, carpenter, athlete) but private, idiosyncratic ones as well (stargazer, people watcher, tchotchke collector, *Perry Mason* rerun fan).

Once you've identified several areas of expertise from your lists, select one to write about. At the top of a blank page, write "I know" then begin writing, as fast as you can, everything you know about this job, hobby, field, or identity. Don't be shy. You may have been taught, as I was, that it's impolite to toot your own horn, to brag about how much you know about something. Go ahead, do it anyway. Write about the big things and the little things. Fill the page with details. The purpose of this exercise is to remind you of how much you know, to prompt you to write from a position of knowledge, authority, and expertise. (Humility will come later when we write about what we don't know.)

THE INSIDE SCOOP

An expert knows something from the inside out. Her view is the insider's view. She knows the language of her vocation, specific tools and accoutrements, the look and feel and even the smell of the workplace, details a casual observer couldn't possibly know. When you write from the insider's viewpoint, you not only write yourself more deeply into your life's work but also supply what Lee Gutkind, the editor of the literary journal *Creative Nonfiction*, calls the "intimate and knowing" detail that will take a reader into that world. What do you know about your life's work from the inside out? What details could you include that would take a reader inside your world? As you write about your area of expertise, write from the insider's viewpoint. Give the inside scoop.

Tools of the trade

Begin with specific terms associated with your occupation or an activity or subject with which you're familiar. The terms might be the physical tools used in your trade or simply specific names of things found within your field of expertise. A surgeon might list scalpels, forceps, hemostats, rubber gloves, surgical masks, retractors. A trapeze artist's list could include midair catches, knee hangs, bird's-nest positions, plunges. A Pacific Northwest hiker might list wild ginger, Pacific bleeding hearts, twisted stalk, vanilla leaf.

Such use of intimate and knowing detail is a gift to readers, allowing them an insider's view into the world of your work. Reading an article written by a high-rise window washer, I learn names for windows I never knew existed: belt windows, tilt-ins, sliders, switchers, nonswitchers. And reading *The Undertaking* by Thomas Lynch—a poet, essayist, and funeral director—I not only learn the difference between a casket and a coffin, but also glimpse a startling array of possibilities: pink caskets; blue caskets; caskets made of oak, mahogany, bronze, copper, stainless steel, cherry maple, particleboard, and even cardboard boxes like the kind large appliances come in. Also on hand are caskets with *The Last Supper* images on them and caskets with roses or sheaves of wheat on the handles. The linings, according to Lynch, are "velvet or crepe or linen or satin, in all different colors, tufted or ruffled or tailored plain. You get pretty much what you pay for."

Sometimes the terms associated with a job or subject

form what amounts to a whole new language, an insider's code. To a New York City policeman, a perpetrator is a *perp* or a *skell* or a *mope*, and an arrest is a *pinch* or a *collar*; to *moosh* is to shove in the face. And anyone who's spent time in a mental hospital has probably learned a language like the one Lauren Slater describes in *Prozac Diary*, "words like *sharps* and *checks* and *rounds*, and then the longer, arcane phrases and words that every patient picks up— *trichotillomania* and *waxy flexibility*, *Munchhausen's* and *borderlines*."

As you give the inside scoop, don't hesitate to be technical, to include terms that outsiders might not be familiar with. If you decide to share what you've written, you can always target a specialized audience, one that's familiar with the language you're using, or you can assume that a more general audience will be able to follow, through context clues, the overall gist of what you're saying. I rarely understand every term I encounter in a novel about high finance or World War II aircraft or complicated medical procedures, but that doesn't keep me from entering the worlds of those novels. The "intimate and knowing detail" that includes technical terminology and insider's codes not only convinces me this specialized world actually exists, but also makes me feel, for a while at least, that I am an insider too.

The importance of sensory details

Once you've named the things associated with your expertise and begun to use the particular language of this world, go a step further by describing this world in specific and sensory detail. What sights, sounds, smells, tastes, and textures are associated with your life's work?

Begin with what your eyes see. In her essay "At Herring Cove," writer and beachcomber Mary Oliver not only lists specific objects that wash up on the beach (sea clams, whelks, drills, jingles, and razor clams) but also describes these objects using details that help the reader visualize the scene: "Mussels holding on with their long beards to stones or each other" and "dead gannet with tiny ivory-colored lice crawling over its snowy head and around its aster-blue eyes."

Next, describe the smell of your workplace: the oily smell of turpentine and axle grease, the acrid sharpness of ammonia, the scent of October wind on the preschoolers' jackets as they run in from recess.

Taste is closely connected with smell. What do you taste in the air of your pottery studio, your woodworking shop, or the donut shop where you work each morning? If your avocation involves actual tasting, describe the physical sensations, as Gretchen Legler does when she describes the taste of morel mushrooms as "barky and buttery and sweet like iron." "They taste," she writes, "like the forest."

Reach out and touch the things associated with your life's work. How does it feel to wrestle a jackhammer or give a sponge bath to a paraplegic? Describe the textures of your world—the cold smooth metal of the examining table; the itchy wools you measure and cut at the fabric store; the wet, warm pizza dough you punch down with your fists.

Finally, describe sounds from your life's work. If you're a runner, you might include the slap of athletic shoes against the pavement, the hum of distant traffic, keys jingling on your Velcro armband, the whine of a neighbor's saw. Try putting all the sounds together to form what amounts to a musical composition, as surgeon Richard Selzer does in his essay "The Knife":

> There is sound, the tight click of clamps fixing teeth into severed blood vessels, the snuffle and gargle of the suction machine clearing the field of blood for the next stroke, the litany of monosyllables with

which one prays his way down and in: *clamp*, *sponge*, *suture*, *tie*, *cut*.

The dance of work

Each vocation and avocation creates not only its own musical score but its own dance as well, a ballet of gesture, movement, and process. Some are physical dances, while others are intellectual or psychological processes. Consider the various actions associated with your line of work. What are the steps you follow, for instance, in determining the best course of action to help a junior high student who is failing every subject? How do you go about locating an affordable nursing facility for an aging parent? How do you take the vision of a home that exists only in your dreams and carry it through all the steps necessary to build a house made of bricks and mortar?

If your work involves physical motions, describe these motions in detail, using strong verbs to paint a word picture. In the passage quoted above, Selzer mentions, among other verbs, *suture*, *tie*, and *cut*. A surgeon also grasps, tugs, separates, slices, palms, cracks, saws, snips, and scrubs, to mention only some movements he might do.

What are the physical movements involved in fly-fishing, juggling, woodworking, or delivering calves? I recently read an intriguing account of workers in a bagel factory. Their tasks included dumping dough loops into boiling cauldrons, fishing the dough out with wire scoops as big as shovels, flinging the loops down steel gullies, placing the boiled rings onto wood slats, then shoving them into the ovens. Before I read the piece, I'd never realized how intricate a dance is involved in producing the bagels I buy at the local supermarket, nor how skilled even the most "unskilled" laborer must be to perform his task well.

This points to an added bonus of writing about your life's work. When you describe in detail the jobs you do, or have done in the past, or tasks you've witnessed others performing, you help celebrate the varied dances of our world, all the complicated steps it takes to keep our planet spinning. As I write these words, someone somewhere is engaged in a corporate merger, someone is sweeping the city streets, someone is shooting a made-for-TV movie, and someone is hauling a neighborhood's garbage away. Tomorrow morning while I'm still asleep, a host of workers will already be hard at work stitching leather soles onto hiking boots, placing a compress on a patient's forehead, planting a row of soybeans, digging a grave for a stillborn child. Only 5 A.M., and already so many dances begun.

The scenic view

Another way to give readers the inside scoop is to describe particular scenes you've encountered in your life's work. First, imagine your surroundings: a school cafeteria, a laboratory, a water treatment plant. Then mentally place yourself in the scene. Look around. What do you see? Who else is in the scene with you? You can describe the scene in past tense, or you can write it in present tense as though it is happening now. Either way, what you're aiming for is an insider's view, a view described by someone who is on intimate terms with the scene. It may help to position yourself in a particular vantage point, as Gretchen Legler does in the opening to her essay "Wolf":

> I am deer hunting, twenty feet up in an icy popple tree that is covered with frozen rain. My hands ache. The wind burns my face. I feel the unmasked skin around my eyes pucker and crack. All my senses are alert for movement in the woods. A leaf sails down to the ground, startling me. A woodpecker lands on a branch within my reach and pokes at a tree limb, rat-tat-tat. The sound echoes in the frozen air.

Notice that Legler not only describes a particular scene from a particular vantage point but also uses sensory detail to make that scene come alive. Reading it, I almost feel the sting of the cold wind and hear the woodpecker's staccato punctuation. My senses, too, are on alert. Though I've never been deer hunting or perched high in a popple tree, because Legler describes a particular scene in sensory detail, the scene feels real to me. As does the scene at the community learning center where Cecile Goding once taught, a center she describes, in her essay "Convalescents From Somewhere," as a "one-room school for adults," a room both noisy and messy. Imagine that you're the teacher in charge; this should be easy, since Goding addresses you directly, leading you into the insider's circle:

Say it is 9 A.M., and you've settled down with the New Readers Discussion Group. You want to shake out something in Art that might connect with Life, and here shouts someone from another corner putting in his two cents. Lucky for us that our classroom is spacious—larger than Mrs. Hamilton's whole house—and as lessons progress, we dance the tables, chairs, and couches around or away from each other. Someone says, "Hold it down over there." Someone says, "Pick up that phone, before I go crazy."

Later on, Goding paints word portraits of particular students so that by the end of the essay we feel as though we know these characters intimately—their names, voices, fears, and desires, as well as the fears and desires of the teacher. Think of writing about your life's work as taking a scenic journey into the world of that work. Describe the places where you find yourself, the people you meet. Give us the insider's view.

A day in the life
If someone were to ask you what you do all day, what would you answer? Could you describe a typical "day in

the life" scenario? In chapter three, I discussed the value of keeping a daily record of your comings and goings. Consider also using the diary method for recording the details of your life's work. If you write for several weeks, months, or even years, tracking your day-by-day journey as, say, a plumber or a graduate student or a new mother, the entries will form a cumulative view of your vocation, a view that might later form the basis for an essay, poem, story, or article.

Be specific as you list your tasks, and don't forget to include unforeseen events, interruptions, and setbacks that occur throughout your days. These, too, are part of the "intimate and knowing detail" of your life's work: the assistant who accidentally knocks over the bucket of paint you've just carefully mixed from twelve separate pigments; the student who breaks out in measles on the class trip to Washington, DC; the fire alarm that goes off every thirty minutes while you're conducting a daylong yoga workshop on the benefits of relaxation. You might even record your activities in an hour-by-hour or minute-by-minute schedule that suggests the pace of your days.

A variation of this technique is to write about a particular day that stands out in your memory—your first day on the job, perhaps; or the day when you decided that you just weren't cut out for this work, that you couldn't last one more week without jumping out the window or strangling your boss.

Better yet, choose a day that stopped you in your tracks, that reminded you of just why you chose this life's work to begin with. In my quarter of a century as a teacher, several such days stand out. The most memorable was a rainy March day nearly twenty years ago, in a fifth-period English class at an inner-city high school where I'd struggled all semester with a class of unresponsive students; nothing, or so it seemed, could rouse them from their collective stupor. Most apathetic of all was a tall, dark-eyed sophomore who astonished me one afternoon by suddenly standing up beside his desk in the back of the room (where, I mistakenly assumed, he'd been sleeping all semester) and reciting not just the thirty lines of James Weldon Johnson's "The Creation" I'd assigned the week before, but the entire poem, in a rich baritone that filled the classroom and rolled out into the hallway.

The tables were turned: Now it was I who was speechless. For the remaining minutes of fifth period, until the bell screamed us back into reality, I sat at my desk and wept quietly, joyfully. *This is what it's all about*, I remember thinking. *This is why I'm a teacher.*

OTHER WRITING STANCES TO TRY
The beginner
Write about a job you've just taken, a role you've recently assumed, or a field of study that's new to you. You're a first-time father, perhaps, or a fledgling nurse's assistant, or your brother-in-law just hired you to frame houses. You have more questions than answers, and the questions, you fear, are all stupid ones. Go ahead: Ask the questions in writing. Better yet, confess your gaffes. Describe the roof shingles you put on backward, the diaper that slid off your newborn son, the patient's dentures that slipped from your hand and shattered onto the hospital floor. But while you're at it, don't forget to express your beginner's excitement about all the new things you're learning.

The duck out of water
How did you land here? This job is not what you'd planned, certainly not what the college aptitude tests tried to steer you toward. Yet here you are, perennially out of place: an ambulance driver who's afraid of blood, a five-foot-two salesman at the "big and tall" men's shop, a landscape archi-

tect allergic to grass. Rather than concluding you have nothing to say because you aren't suited to your job, think of your uncomfortable stance as the key into the writing. True, your workdays might be miserable, but think of all that raw material just waiting to be mined.

The critic

You tried a line of work, gave it your best shot, but finally decided that you simply couldn't buy into it. Maybe you discovered corruption at the center of the trade, or maybe, somewhere along the way, you realized that the career just wasn't worth your while. Where did the work rub you the wrong way? Detail the problems. Suggest solutions. Think of your dissatisfaction as the sand in the oyster, the pebble in your shoe, the irritant that forces you to act.

The late bloomer

Grandma Moses was seventy-six when she painted her first picture. Sam Keen was almost sixty-two when he began practicing the flying trapeze, a process he describes in his memoir *Learning to Fly: Trapeze—Reflections on Fear, Trust, and the Joy of Letting Go.* His account is an inspiring one, especially if you're a reader who fears it's too late to start over or to embark on an adventure where, as Keen puts it, you might be the "oldest student at the circus." Why not follow Keen's example and write about your midlife career switch or your late-life foray into the workforce, college, even parenthood? Trace your influences, the lifelong journey that's accompanied your search. Your story might be an inspiration to others. And if your dream hasn't yet bloomed, if you're still hesitant about taking the next step into a new life's work, writing about your dream may inspire you to take that step.

The amateur

Amateurism gets a bad rap in our society. "Amateurish," the judges say, wrinkling their noses at the oil painting of the covered bridge that your aunt, or mine, submitted to the Octoberfest competition. In a country of professionals, we learn to apologize for our hobbies, our weekend pursuits, the passion for rocks or country inns or forensic pathology that keeps us up late into the night. "I'm just an amateur," we whisper, half ashamed of the work and devotion that neither pays the bills nor wins the prizes.

But where would our world be without amateurs? With or without formal training, with or without the promise of a paycheck, with or without support, they pursue their heart's desire. Hence, the name amateur, from *amare*, "to love." If you find yourself apologizing for being "just an amateur," stop yourself. Remind yourself of the passion and energy that sustain your life's work, and use that passion and energy to fuel your writing.

The perpetual learner

I started to name this section "The Failure," but for most people, *failure* is loaded with negative connotations. I find this unfortunate. As a strong proponent of the success of failure, I can't ignore my many work-related failures, nor the lessons each failure taught me. In some cases, the work failed me; it didn't fulfill my expectations. More often, I failed the work; I didn't have "what it takes," as they say. Or, when I did, what it took simply took too much out of me. I couldn't stay the course.

If you look back over your personal history, you'll probably find at least one and perhaps several jobs or fields of interest that just didn't pan out. Call it bad judgment, a change in the wind, or failure, plain and simple. "I don't know," you might shrug. "I guess I just wasn't cut out for it." Thus, ballet shoes are packed away in your closet; real estate manuals are donated to the library; poodle grooming equipment remains on the top shelf of the garage. I can't count all the work I wasn't cut out for, but here's a start: piano teacher, door-to-door Avon representative, church organist, secretary, nurse's aide, military wife, phone solicitor. And if I were to add to this list the many hobbies, college majors, dreams, and interests I pursued and then abandoned, my failure resume would be even more impressive.

This isn't to say that I didn't learn anything from these pursuits. Discovering what you're not cut out for is valuable information. (I recently edited the cross-stitch sampler that hangs over my desk: apologies to Susan B. Anthony, whose quotation, which once read "Failure is Impossible," now reads "Failure is Important.") Just think of all the lessons that await me, and all the writing possibilities.

LIFE LESSONS

We read not only to enter other worlds, lose ourselves in time and space, be intellectually challenged, and be entertained by good storytellers, but also to learn things. From how to care for an aging parent to how to find the most succulent mushrooms in the forest. From how to navigate grief and loss to how to make our way across Europe on thirty dollars a day.

Whatever your area of expertise—skydiving, raising three stepsons, fighting fires—you have rich stores of knowledge from which to draw. Use that knowledge not only to relate your experiences but also to teach others what you've learned as a result of these experiences. What lessons can you teach us? What inside pointers can you give? If you've talked desperate people out of committing suicide, tell us how you did it. If you serve nutritious meals to a family of seven for ninety dollars a week, share your expertise. If you understand the theory of space-time or know how to renovate an old house without going broke or know how to get your fourteen-year-old to talk to you about school, pass on what you know. Readers are hungry for such information. List steps. Give specifics. Distill your experience into lessons that we can learn.

Don't overlook any job or field of experience, however strange it might seem. Lars Eighner, who was homeless for several years, shares his lessons in *Travels With Lizbeth: Three Years on the Road and on the Streets.* In one of the most fascinating sections of the book, Eighner details what he knows about foraging, scavenging, or what he refers to as "Dumpster diving." Reading his accounts, we learn where to locate the Dumpsters with the most promising castoffs (college dormitories rank high on his list) and even how to make safe meals from what others leave behind. (Avoid rusted or dented cans; select only fruits and vegetables with intact skin; avoid chocolate; be sure carbonated beverages "fizz vigorously" when you pop their lids.)

Let us hope that neither you nor I will have to consult Eighner's book for practical hints; instead we can apply his lessons to other situations we encounter. Reading between the lines, we can learn how it feels to operate on the margins of a prosperous society; to survive hunger, fear, and public humiliation; and to find sustenance, nurture, and even joy in the most desperate circumstances. When you write about the lessons you've learned through your life's work, you're also writing about larger lessons you've learned along the way.

MODELS AND FORMS

As I mentioned earlier, many professions and avocations possess their own tools, codes, and insider's language. Many also have their own specialized forms of written communication. Ministers write sermons, prayers, meditations, and dedications, sometimes incorporating literary forms such as the psalm or the parable. Psychologists write case histories; teachers make lesson plans and progress reports; lawyers write briefs; scientists compose lab reports; sailors maintain ship logs. Other occupations incorporate menus, recipes, analyses, accident reports, autopsy reports, catalog descriptions, inventory sheets, memorandums, and field notes, to name some of the specialized written forms.

Written forms borrowed from your life's work or from a particular discipline can provide models for your writing, whether or not you're writing directly about your work. For instance, a shopkeeper's inventory form might provide a structure for cataloging family possessions in the family history you're writing, or a biblical parable could suggest a shape for a memoir: "A certain man had two daughters. . . ."

As you experiment with different writing models, choose a model that suits your subject matter. In *Tuesdays With Morrie*, Mitch Albom uses chapter headings borrowed from the teaching profession. Since Morrie Schwartz, the subject of the book, was Albom's college professor and their relationship was developed primarily through the classroom, this model reinforces the theme of the book. In *Why We Hurt: The Natural History of Pain*, neurosurgeon Frank Vertosick's use of the clinical case study succeeds not only because it is a form used in medical circles but also because it puts a human face on pain, thus achieving what appears to be one of the main goals of Vertosick's book: to help the reader empathize with those in pain.

If you're writing a long piece, you might incorporate several different writing models, as Susanna Kaysen does in *Girl, Interrupted*, her memoir of a two-year stay in a psychiatric hospital. To tell her story, Kaysen uses actual hospital admission forms, medication charts, case reports, and interoffice memoranda, as well as excerpts from medical journals, an imagined dialogue between two parts of the brain, and even an explanation of mental illness in the form of a multiple-choice test. The variety of written forms and the brisk, almost frantic movement between them help to re-create the crazy quilt pattern of experience that characterized Kaysen's life during this time.

THE WORK OF THE IMAGINATION

Earlier in the book, I explained how I once viewed my writing life as separate from my vocational life. You may feel that way too. Your writing self, the one that pens stories, poems, and plays, may feel so unrelated to the self that paints houses, balances a client's financial records, tutors second graders, or counsels troubled couples that you see no way to integrate the two. Maybe writing is your escape, a necessary release from work that is stressful, demanding, even exhausting. You might feel that the last thing you need is to reenter that world of work through writing. Not to worry. You don't have to consciously reenter that world; chances are, your life's work will enter your writing whether you want it to or not.

I'm not suggesting that everything you write relates directly to your life. After all, librarians write novels about boxing, Colorado gardeners write science fiction stories set on Mars, lawyers channel the voices of Greek goddesses. But scratch any of these works and you'll probably find beneath the surface pieces of the author's life's work—broken perhaps, and bent into a new form, but present all the same. And if you look closely at your writing, you'll probably see bits of your vocations and avocations surfacing here and there:

• In the characters and plots of your stories, perhaps. (My characters, I've recently noticed, spend an inordinate amount of time scratching at a patch of barren earth or staking tomatoes vines, though I haven't tended a garden in years.)

• In the themes you pursue in your essays. (No, I've

never given birth, but I have fifteen nephews and nieces, and I helped raise a stepson.)

• Even in the rhythms of your poems and stories. (Rocking my friend's baby, playing a Chopin prelude, rowing on the YMCA rowing machines.)

If you're passionate about your life's work, it's hard to keep that passion out of your writing. And even if you're not passionate about your work, details of that work will probably find their way into your writing. Your life, after all, is your largest database. Every person you meet, every book you read, and every task your hands perform will be reflected, directly or indirectly, in your writing. Or perhaps *refracted* is a better word for how the imagination takes the details of your life's work (the factory whistle, the prenatal checkup, the stepladder where you balance to paint the ceiling) and transforms them, through time and experience and the alchemy of language, into plays, songs, stories, and poems.

This process may take months, years, even decades. During this time, you may feel that nothing is happening in your writing life. All you do, it seems, is work. When my friend Norton Girault began what turned out to be a twenty-eight-year stint in the military, he had great hopes for his fiction writing. "I was under the great illusion that I'd be able to write while I was in the Navy. Hell, Melville and Conrad did, didn't they? Well, I soon learned: Forget it. Melville and Conrad weren't in the U.S. Navy, where you're on duty from the minute you wake up until you go to bed, and even while you're asleep for that matter. By the time I retired and was free of my 'life's work,'" he continues, "the clock was running on the time I had left to write about it."

The clock may have been running, but it wasn't stopped. All those years that Girault was working—days, nights, weekends—his imagination was working too, storing up smells, sounds, characters, and events that would later emerge in several short stories and a novel. To this day, more than fifty years since his Navy career began, Girault is still writing and publishing fiction based on those experiences.

QUESTIONS, MYSTERIES, WONDER

Authority shares its root with *author*, suggesting not only that we write about what we know but also that we gain authority through the act of writing. But authority resides in questions as well as in answers, in doubts as well as in assurances, in ignorance as well as in wisdom. In *Art Objects: Essays on Ecstasy and Effrontery*, Jeanette Winterson suggests that what the writer knows "has to be put away from her as though she has never known it, so that it is recalled vividly, with the shock of memory after concussion." In the same vein, poet and essayist Marvin Bell advises his students: "Stop saying what you know. Write into your ignorance."

Write as if you've had a concussion. Write without knowing where you're going. Write into your ignorance. What kind of advice is this?

Sage advice. Writing that proceeds from what we don't understand keeps us in the seeker's mode; we write out of the need to find answers to our questions, calm our doubts, and explore the mysteries of our life. This need keeps us actively involved in what we're writing and may also elicit passionate responses from readers who share similar emotions. When we dig deeply, we uncover not only the "intimate and knowing" detail but the disturbing one as well. The question that keeps us awake at night. The doubt at the center of our confusion. The mystery that refuses to give up its answers. The joy that no knowledge can touch.

As you write about your life's work, share your knowledge, but don't be afraid to share your doubts and confusions as well. What is the most difficult part of your job? When have you wanted to give up?

Question the party line; break down stereotypes. Who says a priest can't enjoy pumping iron at the local health club? Who says classical musicians don't like rap?

Embrace opposing notions. It's possible to love teaching and simultaneously hate it. It's possible to know everything there is to know about digging wells and also feel you know nothing. As the saying goes, the more you learn about a subject, the more you realize how much more there is to know.

"The truly great writing about doctors has not yet been done," says surgeon Richard Selzer in his essay "The Exact Location of the Soul." "I think it must be done," he continues, "*by* a doctor, one who is through with the love affair with his technique, who recognizes that he has played Narcissus, raining kisses on a mirror, and who now, out of the impacted masses of his guilt, has expanded into self-doubt, and finally into the high state of wonderment."

Whether you're a professional or an amateur, a beginner or a seasoned expert, you have much to share about your life's work. Write until you've exhausted all you know: the green and gold of the soccer uniforms; the hiss of steam in the insurance office; the leathery, calloused hands of the mason who helped you build your first brick wall thirty-five years ago. Then write into your ignorance, all you don't understand: the delight, the terror, the boredom, the doubt. Write your own story, because only you can.

CHAPTER 9

FROM "PRIVATE I"

TO PUBLIC EYE

Let's say you've been writing for several months now, or several years. You've been keeping a journal, drafting poems and stories. Maybe you've even completed a play or a novel. You haven't yet shown your work to anyone, but you're eager for response. Eager, but nervous. What if you discover that the work that means so much to you means little or nothing to anyone else?

It's natural to feel nervous. There's a big difference between writing your heart out and sharing that writing with someone else. As Eudora Welty suggests, once a piece of writing leaves your hands it becomes, like a mailed letter, closer in distance to its recipient than to its sender. In this chapter, I'll discuss ways to move your writing from the "private I" to the public eye, including how to become a reader of your own work, get feedback on your writing, and revise your work to meet your personal goals and standards.

CLARIFY YOUR GOALS AND STANDARDS

Once your work leaves your hands, be assured that it will be judged according to someone else's standards, whether that judgment comes in the form of a raised eyebrow from your husband, an acceptance from an editor, a scathing review from a critic, or a yawn from the woman in the first row of the auditorium where you're delivering a speech. So before you send your work out into the world to be judged by external standards, take time to establish internal guidelines for your work. Think of these guidelines as a quality control measure, a system of checks and balances that will not only prepare you to share your work but will also help make your work the best it can be.

One way to establish your standards is to study published work that you admire. What qualities in the writing would you like to emulate? Bare honesty? Beautiful language? Odd or unusual subject matter? Accessible prose? Make a list of these qualities, and test your work against the list. I'm not suggesting that you compare your writing to someone else's but rather that you ask yourself whether the qualities you most admire are present in your work as well.

Another method for establishing your standards is to review standards set by those whose opinions you value. I do this by paying close attention to what a variety of people—writers, scientists, mathematicians, critics, sculptors, painters, dancers, and musicians—say about making and judging creative work. If I hear or read a comment that might serve as a guideline for my work, I make a note of it. Sometimes I even place these comments or quotations near my desk to guide me as I write and to help me prepare my work for the public eye. As I'm writing this book, for instance, these quotations are tacked on the bulletin board above my desk:

Einstein: "Everything should be made as simple as possible, but not simpler."

D.H. Lawrence: "Try to find your deepest issue in every confusion and abide by that."

Jean Cocteau: "Writing is an act of love. Else it is nothing but scribbling."

Jeanette Winterson: "The true artist is after the problem. The false artist wants it solved (by somebody else)."

Isadora Duncan: "If I could tell you what I mean, there would be no point in dancing."

A third method is to prepare a set of questions to guide you in judging your work. Guiding questions fall into three main categories: (1) questions about your personal stake in the work, (2) general questions to ask yourself before deciding to share work, and (3) specific questions regarding the particular piece you're writing.

Questions regarding your personal stake in the writing might include

- Could only I have written this?
- Have I been honest?
- Why was it important for me to write this?
- What have I risked—intellectually, emotionally, artistically?
- Is this a piece I want to live with?
- Have I learned something new from writing this piece?

General questions to ask before deciding to share work might include

- Have I left a door open for the reader to enter?
- Is the writing clear and accessible enough to connect with the reader while still challenging her to make her own connections?
- Why would anyone want to read this?

More specific questions will vary from piece to piece, depending on the form in which you're working. If you're writing a poem, you might ask yourself, among other things, if the poem is musically sound, the line breaks are effective, and the images are arresting and apt. You'll probably pose different questions for a short story: Are my characters believable? Are my descriptions evocative? Is the plot clearly delineated? Essays, speeches, lectures, plays, and song lyrics require different sets of guiding questions.

It's important not only to establish personal standards for your work but also to clarify your goals for a piece of writing. Before you decide to share your work, ask yourself what you hope to accomplish.

- Do you want feedback on the piece? If so, at what stage in the process? Are you willing and ready to hear constructive, even negative criticism? Are you wedded to this version, or are you willing to revise?

- What venue do you imagine—a commercial magazine, your company newsletter, an Internet publication, a family Christmas letter? Will the work appear in print, or will it be shared orally?

- Whom do you envision as your audience—a friend or family member, an editor or publisher, the readers of your local newspaper, the general public?

While you're clarifying your goals for a particular piece of writing, you might also wish to consider long-range goals for your writing life. Do you intend to make writing your life's work, or is your goal simply to write, as Isak Dinesen suggested, "a little each day, without hope, without despair"? Do you plan on publishing what you write, reaching a wide audience, and perhaps even supporting yourself with your writing? Or are you more concerned with experimenting with new forms, carrying your work to the next level, and using writing as a personal growth tool? Write down your long-range goals, perhaps in your journal or notebook, and refer to them often.

Establishing your personal goals and guidelines won't guarantee that your work will be received with open arms, or even that it will be evaluated fairly. But knowing in advance what you expect from your writing will help you better prepare your work to be shared.

DECIDE WHEN TO SHARE YOUR WORK

The issue of when to share your work is actually a two-part issue. The first part concerns you—your skill as a writer, your confidence and humility level, and your willingness to learn from response to your work. If you're a beginning writer or if you're unskilled in such rudiments as proper sentence structure, punctuation, and grammar, you should probably hone these skills before you present your work to others; if you don't, responses to your work may well be negative, or, at the very least, focus on skill-level problems while ignoring the big picture you've tried to paint.

Yet even if you're a skilled writer, you may not be ready to share your work, particularly if your confidence is low or if you're extremely sensitive to criticism. We usually think of criticism only as negative response, but in fact any response to one's work that implies judgment is a critical response, and it's possible to be overly sensitive to positive responses as well as to negative. To be ready to share your work, you must be confident enough to receive negative criticism without becoming defensive, falling to pieces, or deciding that the piece has failed simply because someone points out a flaw. At the same time, you must be humble and levelheaded enough to receive positive criticism without floating away on a cloud of euphoria. You must be ready to listen openly to all responses, sift through them, and apply what you've learned based on your own personal standards and goals.

The second element to take into consideration before you make your writing public deals with the work itself. What stage is the work in? Is it ready to be shared? Though sharing a work in progress can sometimes encourage you to complete it, sharing might halt your progress as well, particularly if a piece is so new that it's still a germ, a seed of an idea. Much of writing's power lies in the writer's urgent need to express what has yet to be expressed. If you talk through a piece before you actually write it, you risk defusing this urgency. The talking, in effect, substitutes for the writing. Energy that you might have put into writing goes into explaining, theorizing, or otherwise talking "around" the piece rather than writing "into" it.

And if you get feedback on a piece before you've fully written your way into and out of it, the piece may become a committee effort rather than an expression of your heart's truth. You may get so many suggestions that you're confused rather than encouraged. As I said in chapter seven, collaborations are exciting, useful ventures. But when you're the sole author of a piece, you don't need so many visions coming at you that you're unable to form your own. And you certainly don't need to be talked out of an idea, insight, or creative possibility before you've even had a chance to discover how it might play itself out on the page.

On the other hand, you don't want to wait so long to share your work that you lose interest in it altogether. A saying attributed to the Seneca Indian tribe warns against telling stories at the wrong time: "The bees will come and sting your lips." Be attentive to your work. Don't tell your stories too early; don't tell them too late. Release your heart's work when, and only when, you feel the time is right.

THE IMPORTANCE OF REVISION

For some writers, *revision* is a dirty word. It conjures up images of red-inked corrections, scowling English teachers, and late-night sessions with coffee cup in one hand and thesaurus in the other. To revise, these writers assume, is to admit defeat: You failed, the work failed, and now it's time to "fix" it. But in truth, revision isn't an admission of defeat. Nor is it about fixing something that's broken. Revision doesn't mean merely correcting grammatical errors, moving a word here or there, or making changes to please someone else. Revision is re-vision, reseeing, reimagining. It's an opportunity to view your work through new eyes.

Writers revise in different ways. Some revise as they go

along, laying down each sentence carefully, considering various options as they write. They stand simultaneously inside and outside the writing, and by the time they reach the end of the piece, it's virtually revised. Others are internal revisers. They carry unwritten work in their heads, mentally try out ideas, discard what doesn't work, and plan in such specific detail what they will write that when the work finally makes it to the page, it's already passed through the equivalent of several revisions.

I occasionally revise as I go along, but more often I revise after the first draft is written. Most writers I know use this method. "I'm not a good writer," James Michener once remarked, "but I'm a good rewriter." So first drafts become second drafts, then third drafts; some work even goes through multiple revisions, often over long periods of time. Thoreau wrote seven drafts of *Walden* over a period of eight years. During the revision process, work can change dramatically. When I look back at early drafts of my poems, stories, and essays (I call them "messays" when they're in progress) I'm amazed at what they grew up to be. That's the way I like to think of revision: as a way of helping my work be what it wants to be when it grows up.

Not all writing requires revision, but most pieces of writing can benefit from reseeing, reworking, and reimagining. Anne Sexton, in a letter to a young poet who asked for advice on some poems he had sent, replied, "I am not a prophet but I think you will make it if you learn to revise, if you take your time, if you work your guts out on one poem for four months instead of just letting the miracle (as you must feel it) flow from the pen and then just leave it. . . . What you sent shows you COULD climb there if you pounded it into your head that you must work and rework these uncut diamonds of yours." Work and rework: good advice for those who want to shape and polish their uncut diamonds.

But hard work alone is not enough. Revision also requires passion and commitment. If you decide that a piece needs to be revised, ask yourself how deeply you care about the piece. Has the writing sprung from personal necessity? Does it deal with an issue you feel passionately about? Was it inspired as well as required? If the answer to these questions is no, chances are you may not care deeply enough about the piece to help it become all it could become; your time and energies might better be used revising a piece you do care about or writing a new piece altogether. But if you decide you're willing to give the time and energy that revision requires, you're in for an exciting journey. Rewriting can be as rewarding as writing, sometimes even more so.

BECOME YOUR OWN READER

If you're going to revise, you must learn to become a reader of your own work. This requires a shift in perspective. While you were writing, you were on the inside of the work; now, as a reviser, you are on the outside, viewing the work with new eyes. You can't do this if you're too close to your work. As I suggested in chapter three, sometimes all that's required to achieve perspective on an experience is time. It's best to wait long enough for your writing to "cool," but not so long that you lose your passion for the piece. If you wait too long, you may not be able to reenter the piece with energy; you may run out of steam.

When you feel you've waited a suitable amount of time, reread what you've written, imagining that it's someone else's work—someone who's asked you for a helpful response. It always helps me to read a piece aloud. If I stumble on a sentence, chances are another reader will stumble as well. Sometimes I read the piece into a tape recorder then play it back, imagining I'm hearing the words for the first time; occasionally I even ask someone else to read the work aloud to me.

As you review your piece, make notes in the margins or on a separate sheet of paper. Underline favorite sections, highlight unclear sentences or passages that seem out of place, ask questions of the writer. (Yes, I know you're the writer, but separating your writer and reader selves helps create the distance a critical response requires.) If you've already established your personal standards and goals for your work, now is the time to consult them. Ask yourself if this piece of writing reflects your overall goals as a writer and if it meets the standards you've established for your work.

Any technique that helps you move from writer to reader of your own work will help you achieve the distance and perspective revision requires. In chapter two, I mentioned the writing "stages" I set up around my apartment. Moving from one physical stage to another helps me shift between different stages of the writing process. When I'm lying in bed with my journal propped on my knees, all expectations fall away. I don't have to look my best or be on my best behavior, and my writing doesn't either. But as I move from the bed to the computer station (the word itself suggests a busy meeting place), I feel the shift from drafting to editing, from private to public, from self to others.

Be inventive with your revision techniques. Create mind games if you have to. Several years ago, I invented two imaginary readers to help me move my work from the "private I" to the public eye; I call them Susanna and Gritz. Susanna is plump, grandmotherly, open, and kind. If a creature could be fashioned totally out of vowels, Susanna would be that creature. She is so soft she is almost boneless. She poses no threat. Susanna loves whatever I write and eagerly awaits my next work. When I write for Susanna, I am never afraid. She encourages me to experiment, to have fun on the page, to write anything and everything I want, in whatever way I want. She is my "private I" muse.

But when I want to move my work into the public eye, I summon Gritz, named for a childhood piano teacher who terrified me into excellence. Gritz is all angle and bone and sharp edge. If Susanna is fashioned from vowels, Gritz is chiseled from consonants. He hisses and spits out orders. "Shape up that sentence!" "Excise that cliché!" "Kill off that stereotyped character!" He holds a bare lightbulb over my pages and forces confessions: *No, I haven't practiced enough this week. You're right, I'm not ready for the recital.* Susanna and Gritz are two sides of my writer self, and each helps with a different stage in the writing process.

THE TOOLS OF REVISION

Alternating your writing tools can help you make the mental shifts necessary to carry a piece from the "private I" to the public eye. When I need to feel close to the words I'm writing, both physically and emotionally, I reach for pen and paper. But when I need distance on the words, I go to the computer to transcribe what I've written. When I need further distance, I print out my draft so that I can view the words as others will view them.

Perhaps no tool has affected my writing more than the computer. The computer quickly and efficiently accomplishes mechanical tasks that not only save me valuable time but also help prepare my writing for others' eyes. With a single keystroke, I can change margins or line spacing, reformat text, alter typefaces, center headings and subheadings, tabulate word count, or effortlessly embed footnotes and reference material into the text. The computer is great for making superficial changes in a piece of writing.

The computer also helps me edit more efficiently. If I need two more examples in paragraph seven, for example, I can add them without having to retype the whole section. With a few strokes I can substitute *horse* for *foal*, switch the order of two sentences, or remove an unnecessary phrase. All the major processes of editing—adding, deleting, substituting, and rearranging words—can be accomplished efficiently on the computer. The first sentence of this paragraph, for instance, was edited on the computer. "The computer also helps me edit and revise more efficiently" was my earlier attempt, but after I reviewed the sentence on the screen, I decided that the computer actually doesn't help me much with revision. As I said earlier, revision is more than changing a word here and there or excising a troubled paragraph. For the most part, the computer doesn't help me make the kinds of deep changes most of my drafts require.

Take major structural changes, for instance. When I'm restructuring an essay or story, particularly a long one, what I need is an overall view of the piece, the literary equivalent of a bird's-eye view. But since the computer screen shows me only one portion of text at a time, my can't-see-the-forest-for-the-trees problem only increases. Sure, I can move through the piece by scrolling forward or back, but this linear technique can't help me visualize any structure besides a linear one. Though the computer terms *cut* and *paste* suggest that radical changes can be made on the screen, in fact the only way I'm able to accomplish major structural revisions is to use scissors and tape (or sometimes pins, which Eudora Welty also uses) on printouts of the text. I need the larger view, not the smaller, page-by-page view a computer screen offers.

Not all timesaving devices actually save time in the long run. My primitive, cumbersome scissors-and-glue technique actually helps me revise more quickly than I could using a computer. And rewriting by hand or retyping the entire text, though these may appear at first glance to be inefficient processes, may not be so inefficient after all.

Case in point: In the mid-seventies when I was writing my doctoral dissertation, I scribbled research notes on index cards, wrote my text in longhand, and typed the final copy—which turned out to be several final copies—using an electric typewriter I rented by the hour. Footnotes and bibliographic references had to appear at the bottom of the page, which meant I had to estimate the number of lines a reference would take, then count backward from the bottom margin. Since I hardly ever estimated correctly, I ended up retyping whole pages. And because the final copy of the dissertation could contain no erasures or correction fluid, I had to carefully edit each typed page before moving on to the next page.

This process probably sounds like a remarkable waste of time, especially considering the laborsaving writing tools available today. At my nephews' school, children as young as five and six are already stationed at computers and word processing their first stories and reports. If I were to tell these children my dissertation tale, they'd probably react with curiosity and amusement, the way I once reacted to my parents' stories of inkwells and fountain pens.

However, looking back at my dissertation experience, I see the value of at least some of that "wasted" time. First, since I knew how expensive the typing process would be in both time and money, I was careful to make my handwritten draft as complete as possible before I moved to the typewriter. This required rethinking half-baked thoughts, checking questionable references, organizing paragraphs and sections, and painstakingly editing my syntax and diction.

Transcribing the handwritten draft into print took the revision one step further. As I typed, I noticed more ways to improve the text. Then, typing these pages yet again, I gained even more editorial distance. By the time the dissertation was delivered into my chairperson's hands, it had gone through multiple revisions, each of which pushed the manuscript closer and closer toward publishable quality. Typing and retyping the same phrases helped me recapture the rhythm and pace of my original draft so that the final copy read as one unified whole. Had I been revising on a computer, I might have accomplished surface changes more efficiently, but I wouldn't have reentered the text as often or as deeply as I did by using a typewriter.

The speed and ease of computer functions sometimes encourages me to hurry my work toward a premature end. Why labor to describe my first taste of wild blackberries when I can click on my computer's thesaurus, scroll down its many choices, and select *bittersweet*. Not exactly the word the poem demands, perhaps, but because the computer has trained me to move effortlessly through writing tasks, I may become impatient when I can't keep pace. If I'm not careful, I start acting the way my computer acts: I begin to *process* words. Sometimes I even lose sight of the original impulse for the piece. My need to write the blackberry poem began, as Robert Frost once said, with a "lump in the throat, a feeling of homesickness, of lovesickness."

But if I take the computer's suggestion and settle for *bittersweet*, the word will slide so seamlessly into the poem that it may look as if it were in fact the one true word the poem needed all along. Unlike a handwritten or typewritten draft which documents the writing struggle, revealing messy crossed-out words and substitutions, a computer-generated draft gives the visual impression of a finished text. Rough drafts can look like final copies, especially when I use fancy typefaces. (I know I'm avoiding the hard work of revision when I start fiddling with the "font" and "style" icons.)

Because the computer accomplishes superficial changes so efficiently, it's tempting to believe that deep changes are occurring in the same manner. They aren't. My flawed poem, even if its fancy font makes it resemble an advertisement for the Renaissance Fair, is still a flawed poem. Revision implies reseeing, reimagining, and even refeeling. The words are hiding deep, like those first blackberries, and to find them I have to stop processing words, at least for the moment. I have to slow down, reenter that childhood moment, feel the Indiana heat seeping into the shirt my mother buttoned tightly for protection against the brambles, close my eyes, smell the muggy July mixture of creek bed and honeysuckle and dog, and crawl into the thorny thicket of memory.

WRITING GROUPS AND OTHER SOUNDING BOARDS

Another way to obtain perspective on your work is to try it out on someone else, preferably before you release the work to an outside audience. This someone could be a friend or family member, a writing teacher or coach, or anyone who can act as a sounding board for your work. Choose someone whose opinion you value, someone you can trust to be not only honest but helpful. What *helpful* means depends on your needs as a writer and your plans for the work. If you're just beginning or you're insecure about your writing, you might simply need encouragement and a few minor suggestions. If you're an advanced writer or your goal is artistic excellence at all costs, you may welcome tough criticism.

Your respondent doesn't have to be a writer, though another writer may be more sensitive to your needs than someone who doesn't write. As the Spanish proverb says, "It is not the same to talk of bulls as to be in the bullring." It's easy for someone who's never been in the writing ring to give you advice he'll never have to take himself. Beware of anyone, writer or otherwise, who tells you what he'd do to the piece if it were his. It's not his. It's yours. The role of a respondent is to respond, not to rewrite. What you need at this stage of the process is what Peter Elbow, in *Writing Without Teachers*, calls a movie of your readers' minds. What drew them into the piece? Where did they get confused? Where did they want more information or less? What images stay in their mind?

You can help your readers by explaining in advance what you need from them. If there's a particular issue you want addressed, or if you have a specific audience or venue in mind, let your readers know. This information will not only focus their reading but will also keep them from spending valuable time and energy on issues that you don't need or want feedback on. Of course, if you're open to all kinds of response, let your readers know that too. But be sure you really mean it. If you don't, you may get more than you bargained for.

There are many ways to get feedback on your work. If you want a general impression on the work, you can simply read it aloud and ask for immediate response. But if you want more detailed criticism, it's probably best to send the work in advance and then meet with the person later to discuss it, or ask him to send the work back to you with his comments on it. You can also share your work with a group of fellow writers—formally, as part of a workshop or class, or informally, at an open-mike reading or other writers gathering.

If you want ongoing response from the same group of peers, consider joining a writer response group or starting one of your own. I've been a member of writing groups for over twenty-five years, and the criticism and support I've received have been invaluable. This isn't to say writing groups are perfect entities. Responding to someone else's work is a difficult and sensitive undertaking, as is receiving response to your own; and despite the best efforts of group members, conflicts sometimes arise, feelings get hurt, and misunderstandings occur. Yet even so, I believe that the advantages of being a member of a writing group far outweigh the disadvantages.

If you're thinking of starting a writer response group or joining one, here are some suggestions.

1. Choose writers who are as committed as you are, not only to writing but also to the group. You need to be able to count on members to show up, be prepared to discuss your work, and take their writing at least as seriously as you take it.

2. Choose writers who are on a similar skill and experience level, so the exchange will be as equal as possible. Otherwise, the more experienced or skilled writers may take on the role of teachers or mentors, which defeats the purpose of a response group.

3. Agree in advance on how the group will function. Set up rules and procedures, if necessary, to ensure that everyone's needs are met.

4. Don't apologize for your work. If it has problems (most work does), the group will probably let you know. And if you know in advance that the work warrants an apology, maybe it isn't yet ready to be shared. Use the group's time for work you really care about and have spent time preparing.

5. Don't explain your work before you share it. If you do, you won't know if the group is responding to the work itself or to your explanation of the work. Remember, if the piece is submitted for publication, you won't be there to explain it to the editor. The work must stand alone.

6. While your work is being discussed, listen, listen, and listen some more. Listen not only to what's being said but also to how it's being said. Sometimes, for instance, when two people seem to be saying the opposite, they are actually saying the same thing in different ways. Pick up on nonverbal cues. Listen with a whole heart. You might wish to take notes as others speak. Later, you can ask or answer questions, clarify points, or just thank the group members for their responses.

7. Remember that most people try their best to be helpful. In doing so, they sometimes leap to the easiest solution to "fix" a piece of writing. But as I said earlier, revision is not about fixing. It's about reseeing. Sometimes the trouble spot is actually a door to new possibilities for the work.

FIND THE SHAREABLE IDEA

As I mentioned earlier, one of the questions to ask yourself before deciding to share a piece of writing is, Why would anyone want to read this? Another way to phrase the question is, Who cares? Who cares about the character in my story? Who cares about my uncle's death? Why would anyone be interested in reading about the homeless shelter where I worked as a volunteer?

Moving from "private I" to public eye is partly a matter of finding the universal within the particular. Yes, a reader might be interested in reading about your personal journey or the journey of your characters, but he's also interested in his own journey. What can a reader learn about his own fears, desires, and passions through reading about yours? What can he extract from your work that he can apply to his own life? What shareable idea does your piece offer?

The term *shareable idea* comes from Michael Steinberg, the editor of the literary magazine *Fourth Genre*. In your search for the shareable idea, Steinberg suggests looking to the question beneath the event and trying to locate the central issue within the narrative. Let's say that you've written about the day your son left for college. You want to share the piece, but you're wondering whether anyone would be interested in your story. One way to test the work is to ask yourself what else is going on in the piece besides just a reporting of personal events and emotions. Look carefully at what you've written. Does a section leap out at you—a comment, a phrase, an image—that suggests that this story is more than just your story, that it might also apply to another son leaving for college, perhaps, or to another father whose son has just left home? Highlight that section. It may be the key to the shareable idea that will bring the reader into your story.

Some writers know even before they begin writing what the shareable idea will be, and they proceed from this idea. Others, myself included, discover the shareable idea only after they've written their personal stories. Angela Tehaan Leone's "My Daughter, Myself" began with Angela's childhood memories of a mother who didn't really listen to her. The writing, as Angela explained in a letter to me, "erupted out of personal need." Angela began by telling her own story, but soon discovered that she was also telling the story of other children whose parents are unable, or unwilling, to listen to them. The essay, which was later published in *The Washington Post*, is an excellent example of how a highly personal story can contain universal ideas.

Sometimes even a seemingly small or technical element in your writing can move an idea from personal to shareable— a switch in your use of pronouns, for example. In this excerpt from Angela's essay, she begins by recounting an "I" experience, in this case a volatile exchange with her daughter, then segues into a "we" experience:

When an incident erupted into angry words between us, I tried to look beyond the pouting mouth, the hard-set jaw. "*Look, Mother. Really look at me*"—I seemed to hear her say—"*I'm scared to death about growing up.*" And when the fire of her words gave way to tears, I folded my arms around her and breathed in the familiar smell of the unhappy child-woman I had been so many years ago.

We all wear defensive postures at certain times— pouts that push away, tensed up shoulders that announce that we know best. But still, if bringing down the barriers is what we want, we've got to try to see beyond the pose to what is really there.

Notice how Leone's move from *I* to *we* brings the reader into the piece and suggests the universal idea beneath the particular event. Later in the essay, Leone uses other pronoun shifts to extend what could have been a strictly personal story into a more universal one. The switch from *I* to *we* may sound like a minor point. But the journey from *I* to *we* (or *you* or *she*) is more than just a grammatical journey; it's also a journey from specific to general, from personal to universal, and from private experience to shareable idea.

Questions posed within your piece of writing also provide clues to shareable ideas. Questions such as *Where does a young pregnant girl go for help?* or *Why did what he said bother me so much?* or *How much would a man risk to save the life of his child?* suggest central issues that readers could apply to their own lives. Once you've identified important questions, you can proceed to answer them for yourself and for the reader, or you can continue to explore these questions, thus drawing the reader into your exploration.

Of course, you don't always have to ask questions directly in your piece, nor do you have to point out, in so many words, your shareable idea; it may rise naturally from the piece. Yet even if you approach the shareable idea indirectly or discover it only after you've written the first draft, at some point in the process it's a good idea to clarify, if only for yourself, the universal issues running beneath your personal story.

ESTABLISH PRIVACY BOUNDARIES

Writers differ dramatically on the issue of privacy, not only what they choose to reveal about themselves through their writing but also what they reveal about others. Some writers eschew all personal references in their work, preferring to remain, so far as the details of their life are concerned, anonymous. Others openly reveal intimate details. "I don't see the point of privacy. Or rather, I don't see the point of leaving testimony in the hands or mouths of others," Harold Brodkey remarked about his decision to detail his struggle with AIDS in *This Wild Darkness: The Story of My Death*, the memoir I discussed in chapter five.

Ask yourself where you stand on the privacy issue. Do you feel comfortable sharing intimate details, even secrets, with your readers, or do you wish to draw the privacy curtain as tightly as possible? What about revealing personal details about other people? Do you claim the right to tell someone else's story as well as your own? These are the kinds of questions you'll need to answer before you decide to share work that contains highly personal details.

You'll also need to consider your reader. Though you might feel comfortable standing emotionally naked on the page, your reader might not share your comfort level. He might find your revelations not only intimate but embarrassing, shameful, or even immoral. Of course, since art is partly about pushing ourselves and our readers into new, sometimes uncomfortable territory, such revelations may be necessary and will actually serve the writing. However, be prepared for the possibility that intimate disclosure might stand between your work and some readers.

Questions about privacy occur most frequently when you're writing memoir, personal essays, or other forms of first person writing in which the reader connects the speaker of the piece (the *I*) with the autobiographical *I*. If you're writing fiction, some readers may rightly assume that you're writing from a character's point of view or about the lives of fictional characters, even if your fiction is autobiographically based. These readers will distinguish, at least to some extent, the *I* on the page from the *I* who wrote the words. Some readers of poetry, as well, are accustomed to distinguishing between the speaker of the poem and the author of the poem. However, an alarming number of readers of fiction and poetry make no such distinctions; they automatically assume an autobiographical connection between narrator and author. And readers of nonfiction can't help but connect the narrator with the author, since nonfiction implies, at least to some extent, a factual context.

Therefore, before you make your writing public (especially nonfiction writing) you may wish to consider the close association some readers will make between you and the words you've written. In her introduction to *Hiding in Plain Sight*, Wendy Lesser discusses the necessity for the essayist's "masterful control over his own self-exposure." As readers, she says, "we may at times be embarrassed *by* him, but we should not feel embarrassed *for* him. He must be the ringmaster of his self-display. He may choose to bare more than he can bear (that is where the terror comes in), but he must do the choosing, and we must feel that he is doing it." I agree with Lesser. As a reader, I need to trust that the author is in charge of his self-exposure, even if that self-exposure makes me uncomfortable.

And as a writer, I must ensure that I am in control of the story I tell—perhaps not during the discovery phase of the writing, but definitely later on, when I'm preparing to make the work public. I recall once being ambushed by an essay I was working on. It surprised me, revealing a secret I hadn't planned on revealing, a secret I had hidden for many years. This turn of events presented a challenge. The lines I draw between private writing and public writing are usually quite clear. For-my-eyes-only writing is just that: for my eyes only. I let no one near my journal, nor would I want anyone to read my personal letters, rough-and-tumble drafts, or any writing that includes potentially embarrassing or "insider's only" details. So, I wondered, what should I do about the essay? Should I simply remove the section containing the revelation? Should I rewrite the essay as a story or a poem, thereby attaching my secret to a character or to a narrator other than myself? Or should I share the essay, just as it was?

I finally decided, after three months of deliberation, to keep the revelation in and make the essay public. By that time, I had interrogated the essay: It fit within the goals I'd set for my writing, it met my personal standards, and the revelation was, I decided, a shareable idea. Also during those three months, I had interrogated myself as well. I'd asked myself, among other things, if I'd made peace with the secret, if I had any hidden motives in sharing the work, and if I was willing to face the consequences of making the essay public.

Questions such as these can help you decide when, and if, to make your personal story public. And if your personal story also contains intimate details about someone else, the questions become more complicated. Beyond the legal issues (books are available to guide you in this area) there are moral, ethical, and emotional issues to consider as well. What are your boundaries? Where do you draw the line? Some writers spill it all, not only about themselves but about others as well. Some wait until someone dies before they tell that person's story. Some ask the people involved to read the piece before it's made public. Some disguise names and events or transform the details through poetry or fiction.

Before you make your story or someone else's story public, establish your privacy boundaries. Interrogate your motives in writing the piece. And test the work against your personal standards.

FIND THE RIGHT FORM FOR YOUR WRITING
"I've just exposed the skeleton of a big squidlike essay I've been working on," my friend Cecile Goding said in a recent letter. I love Cecile's metaphor. I imagine her struggling to

hold a slippery, many-legged creature over a photographer's light table or cutting it open to search for its vestigial shell.

Most pieces you write have an innate structure, but the structure may not be visible at first. If you're struggling to expose the skeleton of a piece, try visualizing a physical shape the piece seems to resemble. For example, a poem that starts with a specific incident or anecdote then moves to a general idea is shaped like a triangle; if it starts wide, with a general idea, and then tapers to a specific point, it's an inverted triangle. An essay with two time periods running side by side is like the parallel tracks of a railroad. A story with three separate segments can be seen as blocks stacked on each other, while a story with three interwoven strands more closely resembles a braid.

You can also expose the structure of a piece by imagining its movement. Does it meander like a river, moving swiftly from one idea to the next? Does it gather weight, like a snowball rolling down a hill, as it tumbles toward its conclusion? Does it keep circling the subject, coming at it from different angles like a hawk circling its prey?

Once you visualize the structure of a piece, you can often revise it so that its natural shape is enhanced. If you discover that a piece has no innate structure or movement, try to find a ready-made form that's compatible with the work, then reshape the piece to fit that structure. Though some writers find formal structures restricting, others find them freeing. Maxine Kumin says of traditional poetry form that "in a paradoxical way, it liberates me to say the hardest truth." Howard Nemerov, in a lighter vein, suggested that the use of forms "keeps you from being stupider than the law allows."

Writing or rewriting a piece to fit a particular form can also rekindle your interest in a subject and renew your energy for a writing project. As Richard Hugo says in *The*

Triggering Town, "To change what's there is difficult because it is boring. To find the right other is exciting." The "right other" may well be a new form for your work. Maybe the story you've been struggling with should really be a one-act play—or a meditation, letter, profile, sermon, screenplay, or song. There are dozens of forms to choose from.

Finding the right form can also help you complete unfinished work and discover connections among the pieces you've already written. Several years ago, I found I'd accumulated several short, unfinished pieces that seemed to be part of a larger whole. But I couldn't imagine what that whole might be. Rereading the pieces, I noticed certain images recurring: chickens, eggs, cherries, babies. I remembered a folk song I used to sing to my youngest sister; it contained these same images. The song had three stanzas, and each stanza had four lines. I wrote the first line on a sheet of paper: "I gave my love a cherry that had no stone." Then I searched through the unfinished pieces and found one that seemed to echo this theme. I wrote the next line on another sheet of paper, and continued the process until I began to see that the song's lyrics could provide the form I needed to tie the pieces together. It wasn't an easy process; it took several months to shape the twelve sections into a whole. But when I was done, I had a finished piece to show for my labor. The song had provided the structure I needed to complete the work I'd started.

Form also provides an external standard to push against. It's easy to get stuck in ruts, to keep writing the same old thing in the same old way. Form can help you get out of writing ruts. It can raise your writing to new levels, invigorate stale poetry or prose. Robert Frost's maxim "Poetry is made out of algebra and fire" applies to other forms of writing as well. Fire is the passion you bring to your writing; algebra is the form, the craft that helps you shape that passion into a work of art. As writer and critic Jeanette

Winterson says, "It is through the form, not in spite of, or accidental to it, that the most powerful emotions are let loose over the greatest number of people."

As readers, we respond not only to the emotion beneath a piece of writing but also to its shape. Reading Nancy Mairs's *Remembering the Bone House*, I'm first moved by the intensity of her feeling but am doubly moved when I discover the shapeliness of the book: Each section focuses on a different place she lived. A piece of writing that's found its proper form is a delight to the reader. It says, in effect, "I'm prepared to meet you." It says that the author has done her work, not only the work of feeling and imagining but also the work of shaping that feeling into an effective form.

A WORD OF WARNING

When you move your writing from the "private I" to the public eye, it's easy to get distracted. You may start putting the writing cart before the horse, to forget the reasons you started writing in the first place. That's what happened to me during a recent writing drought. I forgot the truths I'd once known in my bones. I stopped listening to the words trying to speak through me and started listening instead to literary gossip, prizes, fellowships, book sales, the Internet, the best-seller list, my own chattering mind.

It's also easy, once our work moves out of our hands and into the hands of others, to start asking the work to do things it can't do. We may think all we need is to write, when what we really need is something else entirely. Attention. Adulation. Fame. Maybe we want to get back at someone who hurt us, or we need to prove, through our work, that we are worthy of being loved.

In one of my favorite William Matthews poems, the speaker thanks "my friends, who by loving me freed/my poems from seeking love." When we write out of the need to be loved, respected, or admired, chances are we will not write our hearts out. Instead, we will write what we hope will please others (or at least not offend) and gain their favor. If we fear that others will disapprove of what we write—and, in so doing, disapprove of us—we will not feel free to express hard truths, unpopular opinions, or anything that does not show us in our best light. We'll be afraid to take artistic, technical, or emotional risks. Whenever we confuse the human need to be accepted with the need to write, our motives become suspect, and before long we may discover to our surprise that the words no longer speak to us or through us.

At this point, we have some choices to make: We can stop writing altogether, we can continue writing things that surprise neither us nor anyone else, or we can go back to the desk and try, once again, to write what's deepest in our hearts.

LET GO

"Parting from a work of art is a skill," says Anne Truitt in *Prospect: The Journal of an Artist*. At some point in the creative process, you have to separate yourself from the work and send it on its way. If you're lucky, by the time you release a piece of writing, it will have evolved, as I suggested earlier, into what it wants to be.

But not every piece reaches maturity. Many of the things I write are abandoned along the way, or they get embedded into a new piece of writing, or I decide that I just don't want to work with them any more. Sometimes I realize that a piece has already served its purpose (I learned something, worked through a personal or artistic problem, practiced a new form) and there's no need to carry it to another level or shape it for someone else's eyes. Sometimes I decide that the work isn't up to my personal standards, and I suspect it never will be, no matter how much I revise. After all, *revision* implies that a vision exists that I can work with, and sometimes I have to admit that the writing never had any vision to begin with.

So I let it go.

Meanwhile, another piece has grown up right before my eyes. It's shapely, even beautiful in places. I stare in amazement. I can't believe it's mine. Still, there must be something more I can do with it, something else I'm overlooking. How can I know for sure that it's ready to be sent on its way? "I used to keep bearing down on the work under my hand until I felt it was finished," says Truitt. "I failed to realize that each work had a timing of its own, that in some subtle way it finished itself. Once I had learned to pay more attention to *it* instead of to myself, I began to notice that nothing in art is ever 'finished'. . . . Instead, I learned to catch the moment when a work trembled on the threshold of becoming an entity, and to take my hand off it, leave it be."

Knowing when to release a piece of writing is one of your tasks as a writer. At some point, you have take your hand off the work and let it be. If you don't, you won't be free to write the next piece, and the next, and the next.

CHAPTER 10

IF WRITING BECOMES
YOUR HEART

This book opened with a discussion of the numerous benefits writing offers, and most of the chapters have centered on what writing can do for you. That's one way to look at writing: as a tool to serve your needs. Viewed in this way, writing is something out *there*. The words are apart from you, and you reach for them when you want to tell a story, record a memory, talk through a problem, create a work of art, navigate your way through grief and loss, transform your experiences, communicate your deepest emotions—the list goes on and on. There's no doubt about it: Writing is a powerful and versatile tool that will serve you well.

At some point, however, you may discover that writing has become more than just a tool you reach for. The words are no longer apart from you; they are part of you. What was once out there is now in here. Writing has become your heart.

WRITING AS A WAY OF LIFE

When writing becomes your heart, everything changes. Where you once wanted only to express yourself, you now want to hear what the work has to say. You're no longer interested in "fixing" your writing. You want it to change and grow, and you want to change with it. You and the words are one. You're ready to make a commitment to a writer's way of life.

Making a commitment to writing doesn't always require making drastic changes in your life. Most writers keep their day jobs, not only to pay the bills but also to keep, as my grandmother used to say, body and soul together. It's important to keep body and soul together, to remember that you are more than the words you write. Most writers aren't just writers. They're also parents, children, teachers, accountants, coaches, lawyers, doctors, gardeners, deacons, coaches, Big Brother volunteers, neighbors, and members of churches and synagogues. And few would choose to give up these parts of themselves even if they could. Their vocations and relationships not only define them but also feed their writing life.

In "Bloody Brain Work," Marvin Bell makes a strong case for poetry as a way of life rather than a career. (Bell's essay focuses on poetry, but much of what he says applies to other forms of writing as well.) "A career," Bell says, "means you solicit the powerful and the famous. A way of life means you live where you are with the people around you. A career means you become an authority. A way of life means you stay a student, even if you teach for a living. A career means your life increasingly comes from your art. A way of life means your art continues to arise from your life."

If your writing is "arising from your life" and you're satisfied with the quantity and quality of your work, you've probably already made a commitment to the writing life; just keep doing what you're doing. But if you're dissatisfied with your work or you feel that your writing is suffering from lack of attention, you need to make some changes, perhaps even sacrifices, to honor your commitment to a writing life.

Consider these three options: (1) Alter the writing to fit your life, (2) postpone the writing until circumstances change, or (3) (to paraphrase William Stafford) revise your life. I've tried all three approaches. For many years—as a full-time student working to pay expenses, then later as a full-time teacher, wife, and live-in stepmother—I altered my writing to fit my life. Since it seemed I never had more than one free hour at a time, I limited my writing to journal entries, short poems, and scattered notes for longer pieces I planned to write someday when my schedule became freer.

As you might guess, that day of freedom never came. Though outward circumstances changed—my stepson grew up, my teaching load lessened—other obligations quickly filled the spaces of time I'd imagined would one day be reserved for writing. As I said at the beginning of the book, no one actually *has* time to write; each writer must *make* the time. And each writer must also make a personal commitment to writing. When I finally realized that writing was not coming to me, I decided to go to it. The journey was a long and challenging one, and it's not over yet. Suffice it to say that nothing less than major life revision could clear the space for the kind of writing I needed and wanted to do.

WHAT IT TAKES

A few months before he died, one of my friends, a gifted and dedicated writer, sent me a plain white card on which he had written:

> Go to the desk.
> Stay at the desk.
> Thrive at the desk.

At the time, the advice sounded so simple that I failed to appreciate it. But as the years passed—a year since his death, then two, then three—I began to realize the wisdom and elegance of my friend's words.

Go to the desk
You can't stay at the desk and thrive at the desk if you don't first get to the desk. As Hans Vaihinger wrote in *The*

Philosophy of "As If", "The law of nature is: Do the thing and you shall have the power; but they who do not do the thing have not the power." The power of writing begins within the act itself. Whether you keep a regular writing schedule or go to the desk only when you feel inspired, one thing is certain: You can't write your heart out if you never write.

This doesn't mean that writing only happens when you're at the desk. Though for the most part it's true that writing only gets done by writing, there is one part of writing that gets done when we're away from the desk—call it germination, incubation, or just plain rest. Once the creative process is set into motion, it keeps moving even when we're off doing something else; it's the phenomenon Henry James was describing when he wrote, "We learn to swim in the winter and [ice] skate in the summer." The conscious mind may have left early, but the unconscious mind is working overtime.

Einstein noted that he got his best ideas while shaving. Mine usually come when I'm walking, driving, or dancing. Perhaps *ideas* is the wrong word. What seems to happen during these times is that broken synapses heal, metaphors snap together, problems are solved. The word I've been stalking for weeks suddenly turns and speaks its name; the heroine's face comes into sharp focus. In *The Courage to Create*, psychoanalyst Rollo May calls this kind of event a "breakthrough." According to May, such events have four characteristics in common.

First, they tend to occur in opposition to conscious beliefs or ideas to which we've been clinging.

Second, breakthroughs appear suddenly and with great clarity. (So far, it sounds like a fairly simple process, one that is out of my control anyway, so why not just lean back, have another glass of wine, and let the unconscious do its work? That was my initial reaction; then I read on.)

Third, "the insight never comes hit or miss, but in accordance with a pattern of which one essential element is our own commitment."

And finally, "The insight comes at a moment of transition between work and relaxation."

Commitment. Work. I should have known. If I expect the unconscious to do its work, I must also do mine. It's a two-step dance. "Chance," as Louis Pasteur said, "favors the prepared mind."

Stay at the desk

Once at the desk, you need to stay there long enough to receive the gifts writing offers. I often stop too soon, at the first hint of fatigue or difficulty, before the words even have a chance to warm up. Dorothea Brande, the author of the classic writer's handbook *Becoming a Writer*, would probably conclude that I stop too soon in an unconscious attempt to avoid pain and to protect myself against failure. Brande's theory of pain avoidance, which she sets forth in one of her lesser-known books, *Wake Up and Live!*, makes a lot of sense to me. "Rather than revive the memory of our early failures" and "run the risk of hurting ourselves anew," she says, we do not act at all, or if we do, we often carry our work "near the spot where we were hurt before, and there find any excuse to beat a hasty retreat, leaving the work undone, the reward ungathered."

Staying at the desk means working long enough to push through the initial wall of doubt, confusion, fear, and just plain inertia that keeps you from gathering the rewards that writing offers.

Staying at the desk also means keeping the commitment you've made to a writing life, even when you're not actively writing. There are natural peaks and valleys in every life, and what you choose to do during those times is your individual decision. Some writers retreat; some stoically wait out the difficulties; still others keep working, and the writing becomes, as it did for Melanie Peter, the "lifeline of ink" that pulls them out of the valley.

But even the most dedicated writer—perhaps *especially* the most dedicated—occasionally needs time away from the desk. Our heads can become so crowded with language that words begin to lose their flavor, their power. Or we lock ourselves so successfully inside our writing that we also lock ourselves away from the world outside our door, a world teeming with plots and characters and messy human surprises. All work and no play not only makes Jack dull; it may also render him—and his writing—heartless. If all he does is write, he may lose touch with the other identities that bind him to the world: father, lover, son, brother, friend.

Sometimes, of course, life intervenes with such force that you have no choice but to stop writing for a while. Intense joys, expected or unexpected, fill your days: falling in love, having a baby, building your dream house, taking the trip you've been planning for years. Or difficulties stop you in your tracks: illness, disability, divorce, financial tumult, natural and unnatural catastrophe, the death of a loved one. In times of extreme stress or pain, sometimes your only choice is to hold on, to wait out the difficulty. It will end, one way or another, and when you emerge, you will not be the same person you were before. You will have a new story to tell and a new voice with which to tell it.

To everything there is a season, in writing as in life. There are times to labor and times to rest, for the work as well as for the writer. Individual pieces reach a natural end. They bloom or wither, drop their seeds on fertile or fallow ground. Sometimes a whole body of work demands a break. Enough already, it seems to say. Give me a rest.

If we decide we can't or shouldn't write for the time being, we can still stay at the desk in spirit, keeping our faith that the words will be there when we return to claim them. One of the best things you can do for your writing when you're not at the desk is to read. Read, read, and read some more. A writer who doesn't read is like a swimmer who never goes near the water. Musicians listen to music, artists visit galleries, actors see plays, dancers attend recitals. Yet many people who say they want to write never read. This makes no sense. Literature is a writer's medium, the water in which he swims. Robert Frost likened a poet's growth to the movement of a waterspout at sea:

> "He has to begin as a cloud of all the other poets he ever read. That can't be helped. At first the cloud reaches down toward the water from above and then the water reaches up toward the cloud from below and finally cloud and water join together to roll as one pillar between heaven and earth."

Contrast Frost's view with the view of one of my poetry students, who, when I asked him why he never reads poetry, answered that he didn't want to be influenced by someone else's language. I responded that in order not to be influenced by someone else's language, he'd have to seal up his eyes and ears. The fact is, we are influenced by language every day of our lives: sitcom drivel, advertising slogans, junk mail, sidewalk vulgarities, greeting card clichés, talk show banalities. Literature can serve as an antidote for the babble that fills our eyes and ears.

Since writers are formed, in part, by what they read, it makes sense to read the best work by the best authors. When I'm away from the desk for a while, reading good literature makes me want to write again. A line from someone's story sings out, and I want to sing back. It has been said that history is "breaking bread with the dead," and literature is a similar communion. When we read, we're breaking bread with the community of readers and writers, living and dead. In this sense, we're all participating in the making of one big book that will never be finished but rather will grow and change with each act of reading or writing.

Occasionally, reading fine works of literature makes me feel discouraged about my own writing. When this happens, it's usually because I've lost touch with the reasons I began writing in the first place. When I'm not actively engaged in writing, it's easy to start looking for love, as the popular song says, in all the wrong places: in the eyes of others, the marketplace, the bank account, the literary gossip columns, or the best-seller list. Rather than simply reveling in the beauty of Seamus Heaney's language or William Styron's characters or Ursula K. Le Guin's imaginative plots, I begin to compare myself to them. And I come up short. Why even bother, I think, when so many others have done it so well?

It's one thing to admire the work of gifted writers, quite another to wish you could write like them rather than like yourself. It's like wishing you'd been born into a different family or with a different set of genes. The seeds of your best writing lie not in others but within you. Just as each person is a mysterious blend of nature and nurture, each writer is a mixture of natural gifts and learned method. Even if you could copy Toni Morrison's technique, you could not write her novels, just as she could never write yours. Her gifts are hers alone, and yours belong to you. You can nurture your craft through study, experimentation, and most of all practice, but your natural gifts are just that: natural and given. Accept them, be grateful for them, and nurture them in any way you can, including reading the best literature you can find.

Another way to stay engaged with writing even when you're not at the desk is to connect with other writers.

Besides reading their work, you can also attend literary readings, workshops, and conferences or join a writers support group. Writing can be a lonely activity, and sometimes it helps to be around others who share similar interests, passions, and frustrations. If you're housebound or geographically isolated, letters, e-mail exchanges, and phone calls can help stem the loneliness factor, but there's nothing like a face-to-face talk with a fellow writer when your writing hits a snag.

Finally, even when you're not actively working on a piece of writing, you can hone your craft and refine your writing skills. When people say that writing can't be taught, they're usually talking about writing as *art*, the nature factor I discussed earlier. And while it may be true that the art of writing cannot be taught, the *craft* of writing—the nurture factor—can be. You *can* learn to write clearer sentences, compose more effective dialogue, excise clichés, gather information, correct grammatical errors, organize paragraphs, and in general be a better reader and editor of your own work.

Thrive at the desk

If you return to the desk often enough and stay at the desk long enough, the words almost always come through. On good days, you may get what feels like a runner's high. Infused with energy, you lose track of time and space and feel you can run forever. And even on bad writing days, you can still take comfort in knowing that you made the effort and stayed the course. Plus, you'll have something to show for your labor. OK, so maybe it isn't the liveliest page ever written. Still, there it is: *something*, where nothing was before.

Thriving at the desk doesn't meant that everything you write turns out the way you'd hoped. And it doesn't mean that writing is always easy. Even the most talented, prolific writers often experience difficulties. "It's a very uncomfortable process," novelist Edmund White says of writing. "I don't like it at all." Sometimes, White says, he becomes "like a little wet, drenched bird, and I put a blanket over my shoulders and I try to write and I hate myself and I hate what I'm writing." Still, the words come. Not as quickly or easily as he might wish, perhaps. But they come. White thrives as a writer because he gets to the desk and stays at the desk often enough and long enough for something to happen.

Sometimes, of course, we go to extreme lengths to invite the muse, and still nothing happens. The words don't come through. Despite our best efforts, we just can't thrive. For me, these periods of silence and doubt seem to arrive when I least expect them, often just when I think everything is in place, the stage set for writing to occur. Several years ago, after months of complaining to my writing group (and to anyone in listening distance) that I didn't have enough time and energy to write, I applied for a two-month writing fellowship. I'd been teaching full-time for seventeen years, including summer school sessions, and my writing time consisted of whatever minutes or hours I could steal. If I could just get away, I thought, if I could just get that fellowship, my mind would be clear, my body rested, and I could really write.

The day the fellowship announcement came in the mail, I bought a fresh package of yellow legal pads, five pens, and a new typewriter ribbon. Two months, I thought. A gift from heaven. Finally I could write.

Except I couldn't. The first five days I sat at the desk, terrified. I was afraid to pick up the pen. The typewriter keys suddenly looked sinister, strange. The lines on the legal pads—why had I never noticed this before—resembled prison bars. My words were locked out; I was locked out. In my other life, my prefellowship, prefreedom life, I'd never had trouble writing. Not everything I wrote succeeded, but when a poem failed or an essay stalled, I blamed it on lack of time, I sulked awhile, then went back to the desk the next morning. Once I got the fellowship, however, I had no excuse for not writing, no one to blame but myself. My external obstacles had been removed, but that only made more room for internal demons to gather their forces:

> Why spend time writing something that may fail?
> Why fill pages with words no one will read?
> What if they read my words and hate them?
> Why should I even try, when so many brilliantly
>   gifted writers have already said it so well?
> I'm too old to start something new.
> There aren't enough hours in the day.
> And even if there were, what do I have to say anyway?
>   I've never climbed Everest, won an Oscar, divorced
>   a celebrity, spent time in prison, had an affair with
>   a president, survived unspeakable atrocities. . . .
> And even if I had, the world doesn't need another
>   book.
> Besides, I have nothing to say.
> And no words with which to say the nothing.

If external forces wage battle against our writing, they are nothing compared to the war that internal forces wage. One of the quotes I keep above my desk is from Audre Lorde: "It is hard to fight an enemy who has outposts in your head." External forces, simply by the fact that they are external, are easier to spot—and, in turn, to vanquish—than the forces that attack us from within. Internal forces never show themselves because they're not out there, they're in here—looking out through my eyes, listening with my ears, breathing with my lungs.

On this particular morning, the enemy is Doubt. I can tell by its shallow breathing and whispery hiss. Yesterday it was Competition's booming baritone; last week it was Regret, with her thin childish whine. There's a veritable host of enemies out there—or rather, in here—just waiting to occupy the space reserved for writing: fear, despair, insecurity, envy, perfectionism, shame. The list goes on and on. There are powerful forces inside each of us, forces that are capable of silencing us before the first word is written. We don't have to surrender to them, but we must respect their power. If we don't, if we refuse to acknowledge their existence, we'll find ourselves ambushed from within.

Because these enemies dwell inside me, are in fact part of me, I'll never be able to vanquish them completely. We'll continue our skirmishes. Some days their forces will get the best of me. Other days I'll surprise them, turning their own weapons against them. (Just yesterday I located a sharp fear and put it in the hands of a character, who successfully sliced his way to the end of the story.) "OK," I think, staring down at the blank page or out the blank window or into the blank computer screen. "I know you're there, I can hear you breathing. Come out, come out wherever you are."

I type one word, then the next. Soon a sentence appears: something, where nothing was before. Sentence by sentence the page fills. Writing begets more writing. Meaning grows on the page. Because writing is my heart, I know that eventually the words will return and I will thrive at the desk.

That's one of the best things about living a writer's life: There's always hope for the next piece of writing. When writing is only a tool, a way to get you from here to there, it's easy to give up when you can't get from here to there, no matter how hard you try. But when writing becomes your heart, it beats inside you. You and the words are one; writing is your heartbeat, your joy, and yes it can be difficult at times, but still you want to be around it. You want it so badly that you'll go to the desk to find it—even when you're afraid to, even when you suspect that trouble awaits you there. Where else will you meet up with the words?

INDEX